1st ed 1966.   £8·50

D1643445

THE GEORGIAN THEATRE

THE
GEORGIAN
THEATRE

W. S. SCOTT

WESTHOUSE
LONDON
1946

First published in 1946 *by*
JOHN WESTHOUSE (PUBLISHERS) LTD
49 *Chancery Lane London*

Printed in Great Britain by
DUGDALE PRINTING LTD
122 *Wardour Street London* W1

CONTENTS

Other books by W. S. Scott

THE FANTASTICKS

JOHN DONNE

A CLOWDER OF CATS

For
Catherine

INTRODUCTION

IN THIS LITTLE BOOK I have attempted to indicate the nature of the Georgian approach to dramatic representation through the medium of pictures of contemporary date, which illustrate the type of play, costume, pose, and general dramatic action which appealed to the play-goers of those days. These pictures I leave to speak for themselves unaided by any words of mine, save that I have of course been compelled to supplement the pictures by short historical notices of both Theatre and Players. These notices I would have regarded as merely supplementary, and not as in any way attempts at independent or adequate surveys of the drama of the Georgian period.

The illustrations are all reproductions of engravings from my own collection, with the exception of " John Bull at a Comedy " and " The Effects of Tragedy," for the use of which I am indebted to Mrs. Jefferson Hogg.

April, 1946.   W.S.S.

THE GEORGIAN THEATRE

TO GIVE A short account of the Georgian theatre is no easy task.   Either it becomes a large volume, packed with such an amount of detail that one cannot see the wood for the trees, or it must be a short book, which gives a general view of the period, amplified by sketches of various persons and events of importance to the theatrical history of the time.

The second book is that which I have tried to write ; and I have thought it best to begin with a general view of the stage in England in the eighteenth century, to continue with a short picture of the patent theatres, and then to expand what I have said by giving short biographies of a number of the stars who shone so brightly in the most brilliant period that the stage in our land has yet experienced.

The mediaeval theatre, if theatre in the modern sense of the word it could be called—the theatre of masques and interludes—was coming to an end during the reign of Henry VIII, and the drama did not begin in England in the sense in which we now use the word, until Queen Elizabeth was seated on the throne.

The concept of the theatre as a place where amusement or interest is provided for an audience, without any didactic or moral intent, arose first in the latter half of the sixteenth century. Before that time masques and pageants and interludes were the common theatrical fare, and all of them had some specific meaning or purpose, whether it were the glorification of the sovereign in whose honour they were written, or the teaching of some fact of history, or the expression of morality.

They were, in fact, in the direct line of descent from the early miracles and mysteries, which had for their purpose the teaching of religious truths or canons of behaviour, and were themselves but enlargements of the tropes of the early Christian Church.

With the re-birth of learning in the sixteenth century, however, the theatre took a vast step forward, under the influence of not only continental thought, but also of the classical theatre of Greece and Rome, which for so many years had remained a closed book.

The theatre no longer was felt to be a means of giving teaching or of rendering praise ; a new idea had come to birth ; its purpose from henceforth should be to interest and amuse ; instruction would no longer be in the province of the theatre.

Consequently it may be said that the theatre in England was born in the reign of Elizabeth, and became adult almost immediately with the plays of Shakespeare. The up-rush of Puritan thought at the time of the Commonwealth, with characteristic stupidity did its best to destroy the full-flowering of native theatrical genius, and the harsh repression to which it was subjected during the Cromwellian period caused the natural reaction that was experienced under the Restoration.

Under Charles II the theatre was immediately freed from the repressive restrictions of the Protectorate, and surged forward into fresh life. The King granted two patents, one to Davenant's company at Lincoln's Inn Fields, and the other to Thomas Killigrew's company at the Cockpit in Drury Lane.*

At this time boys were still engaged to play female parts on the stage. In August, 1660, Pepys tells us he went to the Cockpit to see " The Loyal Subject," where " one Kynaston, a boy, acted the Duke's sister, but made the loveliest lady that ever I saw in my life." It was not long, however, before women began to play the women's parts, and in the following January Pepys writes again " To the Theatre, where was acted ' Beggars' Bush,' it being very well done ; and here the first time that ever I saw women come upon the stage." Though it was

* See Chapter 2, "The Patent Theatres."

still usual for boys to be engaged, yet Mrs. Coleman, the first English professional actress, had played Ianthe in Davenant's " Siege of Rhodes " at Rutland House as far back as 1656.

As a natural result of the repression under which the theatre had suffered, many of the plays performed were of a somewhat vicious type ; nor were the lives of the players, particularly of the women, of a very high morality. There was a degree of licentiousness permitted in Restoration drama which in its turn was the cause of the fear of vulgarity which was characteristic of the succeeding period. The mere list of names of some of the better-known dramatists of the Restoration dramatists – Sedley, Aphra Behn, Wycherley – show quite clearly the rather unpleasant type of play which was popular at the time. Fun without grossness, humour without impropriety – these were qualities which did not tickle the jaded palates of contemporary playgoers.

Consequently it came about that in the early days of the Georges the theatre was subjected to a much-needed process of deodorisation, a process which was, however, carried a good deal too far in one respect, though perhaps not far enough in another.

Colley Cibber's account of the management of Drury Lane in his day is coloured with pride, not to say conceit, in what he had managed to achieve. " In the twenty years while we were our own directors," he writes, " we never had a creditor that had occasion to come twice for his bill ; every Monday morning discharged us of all demands before we took a shilling for our own use."

This was of course a vast improvement upon the old days of Rich's management, when the payment of out-standing bills was a desideratum excessively difficult of accomplishment. Financial solvency was not, however, the only quality in which improvement had been achieved from the bad old days. Chetwood, who was prompter at Drury Lane under the Cibber régime, states that the stage of his time was " in full perfection ; their green-rooms were free from indecencies of every kind, and might justly be compared to the most elegant drawing-rooms of the prime quality ; no fops or coxcombs ever showed their monkey tricks there, but, if they chanced to thrust in, were awed into respect ; even persons of the first rank and taste of both sexes would often mix with the performers without any stain to their honour or understanding."

In November, 1711, an Order was issued by the Crown, forbidding anyone to go behind the scenes during a per-formance, in the preamble to which it was stated that the orders which had previously been given for the reformation of the stage had had the desired effect, expressing satisfaction that nothing is " acted contrary to religion or good manners."

Certainly then, there were good effects which arrived as a result of the general cleansing, but it must be admitted that there were bad ones too. To use the words of W. J.

Lawrence, this age was "marked by a squeamishness hitherto uncharacteristic of the British people." The vast majority of the plays written at this period dealt solely with "high life above stairs," and so sedulously avoided anything approaching vulgar humour that in fact they managed to avoid any humour whatever.

Inevitably this feeling of squeamishness – which maybe should rather be called hypocrisy – led to the alteration of many old masterpieces on grounds of propriety. The nineteenth century, contrary to general belief, was not the first time in the history of this country in which a canting Bowdler raised his nasty head.

Garrick himself, though none could accuse him of puritanical hypocrisy in his own life, found it necessary to satisfy the feeling of the age by making vast alterations in Shakespeare's plays before presenting them to the public. His bowdlerised versions made them acceptable to the playgoer, and there were very few either intelligent enough, or sufficiently careful to preserve the integrity of works of art, to join with Johnson in his statement to Boswell that to praise Garrick for his Shakespearean revivals "would be to lampoon the age."

It was not until Goldsmith's "She Stoops to Conquer" was produced at Covent Garden in 1773 that the sentimental drama and the over-purified classical plays were dethroned from the position they had held too long.

A word must, however, be said on the other side. Taking into consideration the general feeling of the public as

FRONT of DRURY-LANE THEATRE.

Italian Opera House, Haymarket.
(Before the Fire of 1789.)

to what they liked to see, upon which after all any manager's choice of play must ultimately depend, it was better that such plays as Shakespeare's should be played in Garrick's cut versions, rather than that they should not be played at all. As Mrs. Parsons pointed out in her " Garrick and his Circle," " nobody in his senses could think that Cibber and Garrick did Shakespeare as much harm as the poppy of oblivion."

The second point of interest about the theatre of the period under discussion is that it was an age of great change. When it began, the theatre was to all intents and purposes that of the Restoration. Women had not long been playing women's parts ; it was still customary for men of fashion to sit at the side of the stage during the performance ; the clothes in which the actors made their appearance were for the most part clothes of the period, differenced only by certain formal additions which served to show the type of part which was being played – a head-dress of feathers for the hero, a crown for the king, and so on.

By the end of the period the theatre was in great measure that which we know to-day. The proscenium arch was more or less what it is at the present time ; the actors were cut off from the public, and the play was performed as it were " in a frame " ; the actors were costumed – more or less – in conformity with the parts they were playing ; while towards the end of the century stage lighting was beginning to be considered as of some real importance.

B

In a newspaper of 1785 we read that the stage at Drury Lane was first lighted with what they called "patent lamps," presumably oil lamps with brilliant reflectors, keeping the light from the audience and throwing it upon the stage. "The effect of this light," says the writer, "was brilliant beyond all expectation. We doubt not the very sensible advantages which the scenes, dresses and decorations of this theatre must derive from this improvement will instantly induce Covent Garden and the Opera House to follow so commendable an example."

Not merely was the theatre becoming like our own in its advantages, but also in its irritations. The lady in front who refuses to take off her hat, and give one an uninterrupted view of the stage, was just as much of a nuisance then as she is to-day. A contemporary journalist writes" The box-keepers at Drury Lane actually refuse permission to any lady in a hat to sit in the front boxes. Mr. Harris, it is to be hoped, will do the same at Covent Garden."

There was one particular matter in which the eighteenth-century theatre differed from that which preceded as well as that which followed it, a custom small in itself, yet symbolical of much. It was the row of strong iron spikes which ran along the front of the stage, necessitated by the frequent riots in theatres.

After the famous riot in the Haymarket in 1738, it was laid down in a Court of law that the public had a legal right to express their dislike of any particular play or of any particular player, and that " the judicature of the pit had been acquiesced in, time immemorial." For a number of years any managerial change of custom was the signal for a riot. There were riots in Drury Lane in 1744 when the management tried to increase the prices ; and again in 1763 when the managements of both the Lane and Covent Garden tried to abolish the custom, dear to many play goers, of letting people in at much reduced prices after the third act.

From the point of view of the audience, there was not much comfort in the playhouse of the period. Backless benches were the only seats provided, and it was a case of " first come, first served." Not for the eighteenth-century playgoer were there any tip-up, upholstered arm-chairs, nor was there any system of booking them in advance. A whole box might be booked for any particular night, but not any individual seats. If any particular seats were required, a footman – or more than one if several seats were wanted – had to be sent ahead to take possession of them, and hold them by occupation until their masters and mistresses arrived.

One other custom, still very noticeable in the present-day, though less so than in years gone by, is a direct legacy of the Georgian theatre. The great weakness of the acting of the period was the lack of team work. While the great stars twinkled and shone, the lesser members of the constellation did so, if they shone at all, with a very dim lustre. The acting in nearly all plays produced at this

17

time must have been uneven in the extreme. This
" star " system gradually became more and more
customary, partly on account of the natural vanity of the
actor who knew that he was the " draw " to see whom
the public paid their money, and partly because it was
financially advantageous, until it eventually reached
such heights that in the latter years of the Victorian age
it was more usual – and more true – to say " I am going
to see Henry Irving to-night " than it was to say " To-night
I'm going to see ' The Bells '."

THE PATENT THEATRES

DURING THE REIGN of King Charles I, six playhouses were allowed in London for the acting of stage plays. The flight of the king from the capital during the Civil War, left the parliamentarians in full control of the city, and they, conceiving stage plays to have a predominant influence in corrupting the morals of the citizens, forbade the acting of plays, and forcibly closed the theatres, with the single exception of the Red Bull Theatre in St. John Street, which was permitted to remain open for the performance of " feats of activity and drolls."

This interference with their lawful amusements was not popular with Londoners, and they were overjoyed when the Restoration brought about the revival of theatrical entertainments. The scattered remnants of the companies which had previously performed at the six theatres, formed themselves into two, under the names of " The King's Servants " and " The Duke's Servants." Charles II built for the company bearing his name, a new theatre in Drury Lane, on the site of the demolished Cockpit. This theatre was opened in the year 1663 with the play " The Humourous Lieutenant," which began (in conformity with the custom of the day, on account of the necessity of finishing before darkness set in), at three o'clock in the afternoon.

The great popularity of this company was due, at least in part, to the renowned Nell Gwynn, one of the first women to perform in public in England. According to Wilkinson, " The Introduction of females on the stage first took place at this period, and the Drury Lane Company being strengthened with Mrs. Eleanor Gwynn, a known favourite and mistress of the King, could not fail of being attractive and drawing great profit and company to the Theatre, which from this time was called, and has ever since been styled, ' Theatre Royal '." A few years later the theatre was burnt down, and a second Theatre Royal arose on its site, after the plans of Sir Christopher Wren.

The rival company, the " Duke's Servants," who had meantime been appearing at the theatre in Dorset Garden, decided that a merger of the two companies would be of benefit to all concerned. This union took place in 1682, and the united company, under the new name of " His Majesty's Servants," played solely at Drury Lane.

Concerning this union of the two companies, Colley Cibber writes : " One only Theatre being now in possession of the whole town, the united patentees imposed their terms upon the actors ; for the profits of acting were then divided into twenty shares, ten of which went to the proprietors, and the other moiety to the principal actors, in such subdivisions as their different merit might pretend to. This occasioned great contentions from time to time between the patentees and performers, which arose to such an height, that Mr. Betterton, in 1693, having consulted a few of the principal persons in the Theatre, and interested several of the nobility to aid them in a scheme to obtain an independent license to perform on their own account, they shortly after had the honour of an audience of the King, who graciously dismissed Mr. Betterton and his adherents, with an assurance of relief and support ; and accordingly a select number of them were empowered by his royal license to perform for themselves at the Tennis Court Theatre, Bear Yard, Little Lincoln's Inn Fields ; where they performed Congreve's ' Love for Love ' with extraordinary success, and for a time carried on the concern with great spirit."

The holder of the patent at this time was Charles D'Avenant, who sold it to Christopher Rich. In 1705 the Theatre Royal Company and that at the Tennis Court united under Rich's direction.

Shortly after this union of the players, a certain Sir Thomas Skipworth, who had a share in the patent, became displeased with Rich's management of the theatre, and gave his share as a present to a Colonel Butt. The latter so much improved the value of the share that Skipworth (a man, it is to be feared, with no more proper feeling than he had sense), asked for his share back again. Colonel Butt very properly refused to return it, whereupon the gallant Sir Thomas applied to the courts for restitution, and by some peculiar means, presumably bribery, obtained it, and almost immediately lost the share again at the gaming table !

By order of the Lord Chamberlain the theatre was closed in 1709. A Mr. William Collier obtained permission to open it again later in the year, being compelled, in order to do so, to eject Rich forcibly from the premises.

After various vicissitudes and several different managements, the patent came into the market, and was bought by Garrick and Lacy for the sum of twelve thousand pounds, of which Garrick found two-thirds.

In 1776 Sheridan and three of his friends bought Garrick's share for the enormous sum of thirty-five thousand pounds, and soon afterwards obtained Lacy's share as well, thus becoming possessed of the whole property. In the summer of 1791 the theatre was finally closed, in order to permit the erection of a new playhouse on the site. This new building was only to last until the disastrous fire of 1809. But with the closing of 1791 the old theatre came to an end. As the newspapers of June 5, 1791, expressed it, " Last night died Madam Drury, who lived in six reigns, and was 117 years old."

Covent Garden Theatre owes its foundation to John Rich, son of the Christopher Rich who was patentee of the

Theatre Royal, Drury Lane. As we have previously seen, William Collier obtained a license over the head of Rich, and ejected him by force from the theatre. Before this, however, Rich had taken a lease of D'Avenant's old theatre in Portugal Street, and had begun to build another on the site. He died before the building was finished, but his son opened it in 1714, and presented his company there for nearly twenty years.

Finding the Portugal Street building too small for the pantomimes in which his chief interests lay, Rich determined to build a larger house, and finding Covent Garden suitable and available for his purpose, began to erect a theatre there after the plans of Sheppard. It was unfortunately necessary to clear the site by pulling down some old buildings, part of the mediaeval convent from which Covent Garden took its name, which had been left standing by Inigo Jones.

The theatre was finished in less than two years, and was opened early in 1733. It remained under the direction of Rich until his death in December, 1762, and then for a further four years under that of one of his sons-in-law, Mr. Beard. At the expiration of that time, being troubled with increasing deafness, which impeded him in his particular work of directing the music, Beard offered the patent for sale, and it was bought for the sum of sixty thousand pounds by Mr. Colman and three of his friends. Before long these partners quarrelled, and an arrangement was come to whereby two of them, Messrs. Harris and Powell, became owners of both the patent and the theatre. On Powell's decease, Harris became sole patentee, as well as owner of the building, on condition of paying one half of the profits to Powell's daughters. The theatre continued under Harris' management until its destruction by fire in 1808.

KITTY CLIVE

MR. WILLIAM RAFTOR, an Irish gentleman of good family, from the county of Kilkenny, fought on the side of King James at the Battle of the Boyne. In consequence of his stupidity in choosing to uphold the losing side, he lost all his property, and had to accompany his defeated leader, Patrick Sarsfield, Earl of Lucan, to France, where he lived in exile for some years. Receiving a pardon from Queen Anne on her accession to the throne, he came to England, settled in London, and married a widow, a Mrs. Daniels.

The increase in their family altogether outstripped their income, and the education of the children was inevitably of the scantiest description. The beauty of the family – though beauty perhaps is not the correct word, for her famous attraction seems to have lain more in her wit and charm and a certain liveliness rather than in classical beauty – was their daughter Catherine, who was born in 1711. Despite her parent's pretensions to gentility, it was necessary for all the children to make their own ways in the world, and at the earliest age possible Kitty was called on to earn her own living.

Not having any qualifications for teaching, there was but one other opening in those days for girls of good family, to enter domestic service as what nowadays would be called "maid-companions." Kitty consequently engaged herself to a Miss Knowles, probably a compatriot, who lodged in a house in Hounsditch opposite to the Bell Tavern. This was a great resort of actors, a fact which had a considerable influence in determining the girl's future.

According to Thomas Young, Kitty was one day singing as she washed the steps of the house. The windows of a room in the Bell, where the Beefsteak Club were holding one of their convivial gatherings, being open, "they were instantly crowded by the company, who were all enchanted with her natural grace and simplicity. This circumstance alone led her to the stage, under the auspices of Mr. Beard and Mr. Dunstall."

It seems hardly probable that a theatrical engagement should immediately have followed, without proof of somewhat greater talent than was evinced by a winning expression and an attractive voice, but no doubt she owed her introduction to the stage in some way through her acquaintance with the actors who frequented the Beefsteak Club. Certain it is she was introduced to Cibber, and that he was

26

so fascinated by her singing that he offered her an engagement at Drury Lane at the extremely handsome salary for
an untrained beginner, of a pound a week.

Theatrical affairs at Drury Lane were not then in a very
flourishing condition, and perhaps Cibber was more than
willing to take a chance. Anyhow, Kitty made her first
appearance on the stage in the year 1728, at the mature age
of nearly seventeen, as the page in " Mithridates, King of
Pontus," a negligible part which was specially " garnished "
with a song for her. She played the part " in boy's clothes,"
says Chetwood, " with extraordinary applause."

Her first part of any consequence seems to have been that
of Bianca in " Othello," on October 28 in the same year,
when she was billed in her own name of Raftor, which she
continued to use for the first two or three years of her
theatrical life.

A Mr. George Clive, second cousin to the famous Clive of
India, became captivated by Kitty, and – some time in
1732 – they were married. The marriage, however, turned
out anything but happily, and lasted but a very short time
before it was ended by a separation.

From the time of her marriage she ceased to use her
maiden name upon the stage, and for the rest of her life used
that to which she was now entitled.

One of the most noticeable characteristics of Mrs. Clive
was her extreme combativeness ; she was more than
ordinarily unwilling to be " put upon." This was evidenced in the famous battle between her and Mrs. Susannah

27

Cibber, over the part of Polly in " Beggar's Opera." At Drury Lane in the year 1736, Kitty was (to use the phrase then used) " in possession " of the part, but the management felt that the mere possession of a good voice and great comedy ability were insufficient for the satisfactory playing of the leading part, which needed in addition a certain innocence which Kitty did not possess.

At this moment, unfortunately, Mrs. Cibber conceived a strong desire to play the part herself, and oust Kitty from it. Kitty appealed to her public in print ; Mrs. Cibber did the same. Though Kitty won, the quarrel became so ludicrous that Woodward wrote a farcical play concerning the squabble, and dedicated the printed version to the two actresses concerned.

But Kitty had a certain amount of sense all the same, for eleven years later, when both she and Mrs. Cibber were appearing at Drury Lane under Carrick's management, she was quite willing to play Lucy to Mrs. Cibber's Polly. " No better proof," writes FitzGerald, " could be given of the complaisance of this worthy actress, whenever the interests of the theatre called for it."

After playing under the management of David Garrick for many years, although with an enormous number of quarrels with him, which, however, were always eventually settled, Kitty decided to leave the stage in 1769, at the early age of fifty-eight. The rush for places at her farewell performance was enormous. David Garrick played in both the pieces, " The Wonder " and " Lethe."

She retired to Twickenham, to a house called " Little Strawberry Hill," which Walpole had given her, where she lived until her death in 1785.   In her memory Walpole set up an urn in the garden, bearing this inscription :

Ye smiles and jests still hover round ;
This is mirth's consecrated ground,
Here lived the laughter loving dame,
A matchless actress, Clive her name.
And comic muse with her retired,
And shed a tear when she expired.

Mr Aiken as Cato.

Mr. Aiken as Lusignan.

HENRY WOODWARD

HENRY WOODWARD WAS BORN on October 2, 1714, the eldest son of a tallow-chandler in Southwark. At the age of ten he was sent to the Merchant Taylors' School, where he remained until he had attained his fifteenth year, when his father failed in business, and the little Henry felt himself bound to hunt about for some way in which he could help to retrieve the family fortune.

The first opportunity that presented itself was a chance to join Lun's Lilliputian troupe at Lincoln's Inn Fields, a chance of which he at once availed himself. He made his first appearance in the "Beggar's Opera," doubling the parts of the Beggar and Ben Budge, later advancing to the part of Peachum. The "Beggar's Opera" was given fifteen times, and Woodward made sufficient of a success to warrant Rich keeping him on after the run was over.

C

In October, 1730, he joined the company at Goodman's Fields, where he remained without a break for six years, going back with the company to Lincoln's Inn Fields in 1736, where he appeared for the first time in a piece of which he himself was the author, " The Beggar's Pantomime," based upon Gay's work, in which he played the Harlequin Macheath. This pantomime he dedicated to Mrs. Cibber and Kitty Clive, since it referred largely to the quarrel between those ladies concerning who should play the part of Polly Peachum.

The following year he joined the company at Drury Lane, appearing as Feeble in " Henry IV, Part 2." Here he remained for nearly five years, playing most of the principal comedy parts. In 1741 he migrated to Covent Garden, but very shortly returned to the Lane, where he continued to play the comedy leads until 1747. He was then engaged by Sheridan for the Smock Alley Theatre in Dublin, making his first appearance there in what was to become one of his most famous parts, that of Marplot in " Busybody." The following year he played the same part at Drury Lane.

Two years later he appeared as Mercutio in " Romeo and Juliet," with Miss Bellamy playing Juliet, and Garrick, Romeo. Shortly afterwards he left Garrick's company, and migrated to Covent Garden, where he spent the last fourteen years of his life. By his death in 1777 the stage lost one of its finest light comedians.

Taylor ad viv. del.   Goldar sculp.

Mr. WOODWARD as BOBADIL.

Bob. *What a plague! _____ what mean't He?_*
Who's there? ____ take away the Bason Good Hostess!

Published Nov.r 2.d 1776, by J. Lowndes & Partners

Geo. Taylor del.   Publishd June 3d 1776 by Thomas &c other Proprietors.   J.Taylor sculp

M.ʳ WOODWARD *in the Character of* MARPLOT.

"There he goes."

DAVID GARRICK

IN DAVID GARRICK we see the actor who disputes with Edmund Kean the honour of first place on the English stage.

Born in 1717 at Hereford of a Huguenot father of the blood of the de la Rochefoucaulds, and an Irish mother, he was originally intended for the army, his father's profession, but owing to that father's death, he turned his attention to the law. After his school education at Lichfield was finished, he came up to London in the same coach with the afterwards celebrated Dr. Samuel Johnson ; the one to enter himself as a student of the Temple, and the other to endeavour to make a place for himself in the world of letters.

Feeling himself unsuited for the legal profession, he procured an engagement on the stage, where he made his first appearance at Goodman's Fields under the management of Henry Giffard, in a pantomime, and anonymously. Acting on Giffard's advice, he went for a " trial run " in the provinces under the name of Lyddal, and returned to London, where he appeared, (under his own name this time), as Richard III, again at Goodman's Fields.

The play-bill announcing this performance, ran as follows : " October 19, 1741. Goodman's Fields. At the late Theatre in Goodman's Fields, this day will be performed a Concert of Vocal and Instrumental Music, divided into two parts. Tickets at Three, Two, and One Shilling. N.B. Between the two parts of the Concert will be presented an Historical Play, called the Life and Death of KING RICHARD THE THIRD, The part of KING RICHARD by a Gentleman (Who never appeared on any stage)."

The claim that Garrick never before appeared on any stage is of course untrue ; one must charitably suppose it meant " under his own name."

His success was immediate and enormous. " Richard III " ran for seven nights, playing to houses crammed with all the rank and fashion of London. It was succeeded by several unimportant plays, and some three months later he made his second great " hit " in " The Rehearsal," in which he played the part of Bayes. In this play he introduced imitations of a large number of his brother actors, thereby causing enormous resentment. His good taste soon put an end to these imitations, when he saw how much anger they caused, and the following month he appeared in what was later to be his greatest part, that of King Lear.

His success in this and other parts at Goodman's Fields led to such large audiences making their way to this little theatre, that the managers of the patent theatres began to fear for their rights, so the law was set to work, and Goodman's Fields Theatre was closed.

Garrick now joined the company at Drury Lane, under the management of Fleetwood, and arranged to make his first appearance there in the autumn of 1742. In the meantime he had the summer before him, so in the company of Peg Woffington, to whom he lost his heart, he went to Dublin, and appeared for a short season at the Smock Alley house, playing Richard III and Hamlet.

On June 4 he appeared in the latter part, with Peg Woffington as Ophelia. He had made a number of alterations in the play from what had long been traditional, among other things dispensing with the usual musical accompaniment to Hamlet's entrances. The altered play was such a success that he received a number of requests that it should be repeated, and in consequence he played it several times.

It may be of interest that the alterations which Hamlet required occupied a great deal of his mind throughout his stage career.

Thirty years later we find him writing to Sir W. Young on the subject, as follows :

Jan. 10, 1776.

I have ventured to produce 'Hamlet,' with alterations. It was the most imprudent thing I ever did in all my life ; but I had sworn I would not leave the stage till I had rescued that noble play from all the rubbish of the fifth act. I have brought it forth without the Grave-digger's trick and the fencing-match. The alteration was received with general approbation, beyond my most warm expectations.

One must applaud his interest, though hardly approve his actions !

On October 5 he appeared for the first time at Drury Lane, playing his old Goodman's Fields parts, as well as those he played in Dublin. While playing at the Lane, he, his friend Macklin, and Peg Woffington set up a ménage à trois. Owing to rivalry for Peg's affections, however, they quarrelled, and the attempt to share a house came to an end.

In 1744 came the final rupture with Peg Woffington, who had been by way of being engaged to Garrick, and their presents to each other were returned, David keeping, however, a very fine pair of diamond buckles. This fact has constantly been used to back up a charge of meanness against him, but it is more than probable that he retained them merely as a memento of a connection that had at one time been a happy one.

After a second highly successful visit to Dublin, Garrick accepted an offer to play on sharing terms at Covent

Garden, where he appeared in a number of parts, among them Richard III, Othello, and Macbeth.

Lacy, who had succeeded Fleetwood as manager of the Lane, was beginning to find it rather too much of a burden to deal with alone, and Garrick offered to buy a partnership for the sum of eight thousand pounds. Lacy joyfully agreed, and at the beginning of the 1747-8 season Garrick found himself joint-manager of Drury Lane.

About this time he had met, and been captivated by a young German dancer, known as La Violetta, rumoured to be an illegitimate daughter of Lord Burlington. After three years' courtship he married her, and their marriage proved exceptionally happy. During the thirty years that elapsed before his death they were said never to have spent one day apart. She survived her husband by over forty years, being buried by his side in Westminster Abbey at the remarkable age of ninety-nine, and talking to the last of her " dear Davy."

Garrick's successes during the remaining thirty years of his life were so many that it would be tedious to treat of them all. Let us come to the famous season of 1776, when he made his farewell to the stage. These farewell performances began on April 11 with Abel Drugger, and ended on June 10 with Don Felix in " The Wonder."

He had intended to take his leave in the same part in which he had made his first appearance, that of Richard III, but his health was not equal to it, so Don Felix was chosen instead. At the end of the play Garrick spoke an address, with many breaks and stops. It was said by several who were present that it was more like a funeral than a theatrical entertainment. Sobs were heard in the house, as the audience realised they were never again to see their matchless Davy in any of the parts he had made famous.

The story of his last triumph is well-known, but may perhaps again be told. During a debate in the House of Commons, he was present in the Distinguished Strangers' Gallery. Being a privileged person he did not leave when there was a division, and the call " Strangers must withdraw " was made. The following day an insignificant country member rose to draw the attention of the House to the impropriety of a " rogue and vagabond " listening to their debates. Immediately Burke rose to his feet, to defend the great master of oratory who had taught them all they knew. He was followed by Fox, and a number of others, and the House put on record its sense of the distinction conferred on it by the presence of so distinguished a stranger.

While staying with Lord Spencer at Althorp, Garrick was attacked with the stone, and removed to his house in Adelphi Terrace, where he lingered for a few days, and died on January 20, 1779.

On February 1 he was buried in Westminster Abbey with great ceremony, the funeral procession reaching the whole way from the house to the Abbey.

Of all the magnificent tributes which were paid to his

memory, that of his old friend Dr. Johnson is perhaps the finest. " I am disappointed," he said, " by that stroke of death which has eclipsed the gaiety of nations and impoverished the public stock of harmless pleasure."

As Hazlitt said, " Certainly, by all accounts, if anyone was ever moved by the true histrionic *aestus*, it was Garrick." This seems to have been the universal opinion ; all his contemporaries agreed. We may perhaps end this short account of one of the two greatest masters of acting on the British stage, by quoting the words of Garrick's earliest friend, the same Dr. Johnson who taught him as a boy ; " Garrick was no declaimer ; there was not one of his own scene-shifters who could not have spoken ' To be or not to be ' better than he did : yet *he was the only actor I ever saw, whom I could call a master both in tragedy and comedy* . . . A true conception of character, and natural expression of it were his distinguished excellences."

SPRANGER BARRY

THE GREATEST OTHELLO of all ! that was Spranger Barry.
Born in Skinner Row, Dublin, later to be of " Mayor and
Aldermen " fame, in 1719, he was the son of a silversmith,
and is said to have been descended from the last Lord
Santry.   He was apprenticed to his father's trade, married
a wife with a dowry, enormous for those days, and
comfortable enough even in these, of fifteen thousand
pounds, and had every opportunity of settling down as
a wealthy master of his craft.

But such was not Barry's idea. He spent every penny
his wife brought him in the shortest possible time, and at
the age of thirty-four he not only had one penny left, but
was heavily in debt. He was adjudged bankrupt, and in
order to retrieve his fortunes, determined to go on the
stage. This he did by arranging a performance for his

own benefit, in which he appeared in what was always to be considered his greatest part, and one in which it is said that no other actor has ever equalled him, that of Othello.

During the season at the Old Smock Alley Theatre he played many other leading parts, among them Hotspur, Henry V, and King Lear. The following year he had the good fortune to play second leads to Garrick, when he visited Dublin in 1745, and in Othello he was actually supported by Garrick, Barry playing the title-role.

He impressed Garrick so highly, that he used his influence with Lacy of Drury Lane, and Barry was offered and accepted an engagement there for the following year.

On October 4, 1746, Barry made his debut at the Lane, again in the part of Othello. His success was enormous, and his popularity soon rivalled that of Garrick himself. These two great actors alternated the parts of Hamlet and Macbeth, and it is said that whereas Garrick was easily the greater as the latter, and Barry much the better Othello, in Hamlet honours were easy.

Harry remained at Drury Lane until 1750, when he joined the Covent Garden company, on account, it is said, of Garrick's jealousy of his performance as Romeo. As a result of this, " Romeo and Juliet " was produced simultaneously at both theatres, and a regular duel began, which lasted for twelve performances, until the audiences were thoroughly tired of it, as was evidenced by a little verse which went the round of the town.

' Well, what's to-night ? ' says angry Ned,
   As up from bed he rouses.
' Romeo again,' and shakes his head,
   ' A plague on both your houses.'

On one occasion, to Miss Bellamy's request " Romeo, Romeo : wherefore art thou Romeo ? " a witty Irish voice called out, " Faith, because Barry's at the other house ! "

After some years of playing in rivalry with Garrick, Barry returned to Dublin, this time in management. He re-built the Crow Street Theatre, where he appeared in November, 1758, as Hamlet. Again Barry had a rival, this time not as an actor so much as as a manager, and a battle royal was fought between the two Dublin theatres, in which both managements lost considerable sums of money.

In order to recoup their losses, Barry and his partner, Woodward, opened a new theatre in Cork, which was sufficiently successful to enable Barry to return to Crow Street, where he produced the masque " King Arthur," notable only for the fact that through it the great composer Purcell became famous.

Crow Street, however, was still more of a liability than an asset, and in 1764 Barry handed over the theatre to Mossop, the proprietor of Smock Alley, and after two short but very successful seasons at Cork and Limerick, he returned to London, and engaged under Foote at the

Haymarket. There he stayed for some years, his leading lady being Mrs. Dance, whom in 1768 he was at last able to marry, his wife, whom he had loathed ever since he had spent her dowry, and Mr. Dance, the obstacles, both having been conveniently removed by death.

The year before his marriage, he had been engaged by Garrick for Drury Lane, his former rivalry being happily forgiven if not forgotten, and he appeared in his favourite character of Othello in October, 1767.

For the next seven years he stayed under Garrick's management, playing all his old characters, and in 1774, accompanied by his second wife, whom he adored, he joined the company at Covent Garden.

He died on January 10, 1777, and was buried in the Cloisters of Westminster Abbey, not far from the spot where two years later his great rival, David Garrick, was to find his last resting-place.

Even the bitter-tongued Churchill could not refrain from a comparatively kindly description of this magnificent artist. He wrote :

In person taller than the common size,
Behold where Barry draws admiring eyes ;
When lab'ring passions in his bosom pent,
Convulsive rage, and Struggling heave for vent,
Spectators, with imagined terrors warm,
Anxious expect the bursting of the storm :
But, all unfit in such a pile to dwell,
His voice comes forth like Echo from her cell ;

44

To swell the tempest needful aid denies,
And all a-down the stage in feeble murmur dies.
What man, like Barry, with such pains, can err
In elocution, action, character ?
What man could give, if Barry was not here,
Such well-applauded tenderness to Lear ?
Who else can speak so very, very fine,
That sense may kindly end with every line ?
Some dozen lines, before the ghost is there,
Behold him for the solemn scene prepare.
See how he frames his eyes, poises each limb,
Puts the whole body into proper trim,—
From whence we learn, with no great stretch of art,
Five lines hence comes a ghost, and lo ! a start.
When he appears most perfect, still we find
Something which jars upon and hurts the mind.
Whatever lights upon a part are thrown,
We see too plainly they are not his own :
No flame from nature ever yet he caught,
Nor knew a feeling which he was not taught ;
He raised his trophies on the base of art,
And conn'd his passions, as he conn'd his part.

I end by quoting what Davies said of him.
" Of all the tragic actors who have trod the English
stage for these last fifty years, Mr. Barry was unquestionably
the most pleasing. Since Booth and Wilks, no actor
had shown the public a just idea of the hero or the lover ;

Barry gave dignity to the one and passion to the other : in his person he was tall without awkwardness ; in his countenance, handsome without effeminacy ; in his uttering of passion, the language of nature alone was communicated to the feelings of an audience."

Mrs. Woffington

Jᵒ. Marchand, sculp.

Engraved by Pearson from an original Painting by Eckhart, in the possession of Charles Pollard Esquire

Mrs WOFFINGTON.

PEG WOFFINGTON

PROBABLY THE MOST fascinating of all the actresses of her century was the lovely Peg Woffington. Her father, John Woffington, was a bricklayer in Dublin, who died in 1720, leaving a widow and two tiny children. As he left them entirely destitute, Mrs. Woffington set up in business as a huckster on Ormonde Quay, but her lack of capital caused the business to fail, and she was reduced to hawking fruit and watercress in the streets, in the manner of the legendary Molly Malone in " Dublin's fair city," who

" Wheeled her wheel-barrow
   Through streets broad and narrow,
      Crying ' Cockles and mussels, alive, alive-O.' "

In a booth near College Green, a certain Frenchwoman used to exhibit feats of strength and agility, one of which was to cross the stage on a tight-rope, with a basket hanging

47

D

from each foot, each basket containing a small child. One of the infants who undertook the perilous journey for the sake of the few pence reward, was the little Peg.

Mercifully, for the sake of the human freight carried in this perilous trick, the experiment failed ; presumably the Dublin public did not care to see babies take such risks, even in the callous days of the 1720s, or maybe the supply of suitable children ran out ; whatever it was, Peg was soon back on the ground again, earning her living by assisting her mother as a hawker of vegetables.

When she reached the age of ten, she was offered another engagement by the same enterprising manageress, who after the failure of her tight-rope act, had started a theatrical company of children, presumably in imitation of Rich's company in Lincoln's Inn fields, in which Harry Wood-ward made his first successes. In this Lilliputian Company Peg starred in the part of Polly in " The Beggar's Opera," as well as playing Nell in " The Devil to pay."

The remarkable ability that she showed at her tender age attracted the attention of Thomas Elrington, who was manager of the Aungier Street Theatre, from whom she received an engagement to play various adult parts, as well as to entertain the audience by dancing between the acts. For some seven or eight years she remained a member of one or other of the Dublin companies, making herself popular with Dublin audiences, not only at Aungier Street, but also at the Rainsford Street Theatre, and the famous Smock Alley House.

At the latter theatre she made her first considerable success in a tragedy part, that of Ophelia, which she first played in April, 1737. Three years later she appeared for the first time in what to the end of her life was considered her finest part, in which she excelled all others, that of Sir Harry Wildair in Farquhar's " Constant Couple."

Rumours of her exquisite performance as Wildair reached Rich in London, who wasted no time in offering her an engagement at Covent Garden, which she at once accepted. Her meeting with Rich on her arrival at the theatre, surrounded by the five dozen cats by which he was invariably accompanied, is immortalised in the famous picture of the scene.

She made her first appearance in London as Silvia in " The Recruiting Officer." In this part she had to appear dressed as a boy, and her bewitching appearance and consummate ability took the town by storm. Later in the month she played the part in which she had been so successful in Dublin, that of Sir Harry Wildair, and achieved even greater success.

What would one not give nowadays to hear her sing Wildair's charming though improper song ? One can imagine the wild applause with which it must have been greeted, sung by so charming a girl, in the habiliments of a boy.

> " Thus Damon knocked at Celia's door,
> He sighed and begged and wept and swore :
> The sign was so

She answered ' no,
No, no, no.'

Again he sighed, again he prayed :
' No, Damon, no, I am a maid ;
Consider, no, I am a maid,
No, no, no.'

At last his sighs and tears made way ;
She rose and softly turned the key :
' Come in,' said she, ' but do not stay ;
I may conclude
You will be rude :
But, if you are, you may.'

After playing a number of other parts in the same season
under Rich's management, she was engaged for the next
year at Drury Lane, where she began the season with the
same parts as those she had played the year before at
Covent Garden, Silvia in " The Recruiting Officer,"
followed by Sir Harry Wildair. Her enormous success was
repeated, and she added a number of other roles to her
repertoire, among them that of Helena in " A Mid-
summer's Night's Dream " (in which, through illness, she
broke down), and Cordelia, which she played to David
Garrick's Lear.

Early in the summer of this year, 1742, she returned to
Dublin, where she found she had attained to heights of

fame hitherto unknown on the Irish stage. In the June she crossed the sea again, and once more appeared as Wildair at Drury Lane, following it by her first performance of Lady Anne to the Richard III of Garrick.

It was at this time that Peg and Garrick became declared lovers. One of Macklin's biographers tells an amusing if improper story of their liaison. (It was in Macklin's house in Bow Street that Peg had rooms.)

A certain young peer, of a very jealous disposition, having been greatly attracted by Peg, was in the habit of calling on her without any warning. One day David Garrick was in Peg's room when the young nobleman called. As soon as he heard the knock on the door, Garrick leapt out of bed, snatched up his clothes, and dashed into Macklin's room, hoping he would not be seen. He reached this refuge in time, but as luck would have it, left his wig behind him, and as the second lover entered the room, he caught his feet in the wig which was lying on the floor.

Naturally enough, he began to upbraid his mistress for her faithlessness. She listened quite calmly, and told him not to be a fool, but, to hand her back the wig at once. "Do you own the wig, then?" he asked in amazement. "Of course I do," she replied. "I'm sure it was my money bought it, and I hope it will repay me with money and reputation too." She went on to explain that she was about to appear in another male part, and had been rehearsing with a man's wig just before she went to bed; how dare he suspect her?

Garrick heard the story on the following day, and was so delighted with her ingenuity that, as Macklin said, " he gave us a dinner the same day at Richmond, where we all laughed heartily at his lordship's gullibility."

One of her greatest admirers, Sir Charles Hanbury Williams, taxed her on one occasion with having been with Garrick, despite her promise to him that she would see her David no more. She replied that she had not seen him for ages. " I know," said Sir Charles, " that you saw him yesterday." " Well," she replied, " and is not that an age ? "

Hanbury Williams composed a number of verses in praise of the lovely Peg, though some of them show quite clearly that he was not under any illusions as to her character. The following verses are typical :

> Though Peggy's charms have oft been sung,
> The darling theme of every tongue,
>   New praises still remain ;
> Beauty like hers may well infuse
> New flights, new fancies, like a Muse,
>   And brighten every strain.
>
> 'Tis not her form alone I prize,
> Which every fool that has his eyes,
>   As well as I can see ;
> To say she's fair is but to say,
> When the sun shines at noon, 'tis day——
>   Which none need learn of me.

But I'm in love with Peggy's mind,
Where every virtue is combin'd,
    That can adorn the fair,
Excepting one, you scarce can miss
So trifling that you would not wish
    That virtue had been there.

She who possesses all the rest,
Must sure excel the prude whose breast
    That virtue shares alone ;
To seek perfection is a jest :
They who have fewest faults are best ;
    And Peggy has but one.

The Garrick-Woffington connection, however, eventually ended, as was only to be expected, and Peg packed up and returned to her David all the presents he had given her. Garrick did the same to her, but characteristically failed to return the most valuable present of all, a pair of diamond shoe-buckles.

After waiting for some time, Peg wrote and as delicately as possible reminded him of the fact. He replied that as they were the only little mementoes he had of the many happy hours they had spent together, he hoped she would allow him to keep them.

When Garrick assumed the managership of Drury Lane, it was obviously too awkward for Peg to remain, and she applied to Sheridan for an engagement in Dublin. This he at once offered her, and after some bargaining, they agreed on the sum of four hundred pounds for the season. Her success in Dublin knew no bounds, and the average receipts of the theatre on the nights when she played, were a hundred pounds a night.

Sheridan, always generous, and frequently foolishly so, instead of the sum mentioned in the contract, paid her double, and she remained in Dublin, to the pleasure of herself, her manager, and the Dublin playgoers, until 1754, where there were riots in the theatre, as a result of the supposed interference of the Beef-Steak Club in political matters. On account of these riots, Sheridan closed the house, and Peg returned to London, and appeared again at Covent Garden, where she had her usual success.

On May 17, 1757, at a benefit performance at Covent Garden, there occurred the tragic happening which ended Peg's professional career. " As you Like It " was being played, and Peg was playing Rosalind. During the last act she complained of feeling extremely unwell, but got through her first entrance. She came off to the change of costume, and said that she felt very ill indeed, but hoped she would be able to finish the play.

This she did manage to do, and began to speak the epilogue, but when she arrived at the lines

" If I were a woman I would kiss as many of you as had beards that pleased me "

her voice broke. She endeavoured to go on, but her voice failed ; again she tried, but could not get her voice to

54

speak the lines ; another pause, and with a scream of " O God ! " she staggered to the wings, and fell.

For three years she lingered, living sometimes in London and sometimes at Teddington, where she had a villa. Her peculiar sense of morals, however, was not changed by the tragedy of her involuntary retirement from the stage. Despite Charles Reade's delightful story, in which she was made to become a " humble, pious, long-repentant Christian," the truth seems to be that she confidently anticipated a return to health and the practice of her profession. In the meantime she spent the remaining three years, which was all the time allowed her, in living with a Colonel Caesar as his mistress.

She died in March, 1760, leaving an annuity to her mother, and everything else she possessed to her sister, thus (to quote Mackin's somewhat cynical remark) " disappointing Colonel Caesar, as he perhaps might have disappointed her had it been his turn to go first."

JOHN MOODY

MOODY WAS AN IRISHMAN from Cork ; his real name being
Cochrane. His father was a barber, and carried on his
business in Tuckey's Lane, the future actor being engaged
in the same business for a number of years. For some
reason, which history has never been able precisely to
determine, Moody went to the West Indies ; not without
some suspicion arising in his later years that he was sent
there at His Majesty's orders, for his country's good.
But be that as it may, he had no sooner arrived in Jamaica
than he joined the company of actors established at
Kingston. There he spent many years, but eventually
crossed the seas to England, where on the strength of
his colonial experience he applied for an engagement at
Drury Lane.

An engagement of a sort he obtained, but it was only to

play the most insignificant parts of " the carriage waits, my lord " variety, until his broad Cork accent, which he had never completely lost, caused him to be cast for the part of Captain O'Cutter in Colman's comedy, " The Jealous Wife."

His success in this piece was such that even the satirical Churchill wrote of him in the " Rosciad "

Long, from a country ever hardly us'd,
At random censur'd, and by most abus'd,
Have Britons drawn their sport, with no kind view,
And judg'd the many, by the rascal few ;
From thee, Moody, have we learn'd to raise
Mirth from their foibles, from their virtues praise.

He was cast for the part of Major O' Flaherty in " The West Indian," a part of a similar type to that in which he made his first success. He seems to have made a decided hit, as a contemporary notice says " he has supported this character with such judgment and masterly execution as to divide applause with the author by making a sub-ordinate character (though not the hero of the fable) the hero of the audience."

58

THOMAS KING

KING IS PERHAPS more worthy of remembrance as an eighteenth-century actor by virtue of his remarkably high moral character than of his ability in his chosen profession, though that was considerable enough.

He was born of a respectable family in the north of England, and educated at a grammar school in his native town, but was soon captivated by the stage, and like the generality of enthusiasts who determined to make it their profession, he began by taking an engagement in a small touring company.

The repute in which such companies were held is seen from the following description by a contemporary, who wrote of King after he became well-known, " His parents, (which is too common a fault) behaved incautiously. Instead of endeavouring to reclaim him from such a pursuit by gentle methods, and a remission of the first offence, at once abandoned him to his fortune, as if there was a talismanic power in the profession, that marked its votaries with reprobation for life. Thus thrown on the world at an early age, he rambled about the country, subject to all these awkward distresses and adventures, that are inseparable from this kind of life. To one of his sprightly cast and sensible turn of mind, these adventures were serviceable. It presented to his view a number of undisguised characters he could never otherwise have met with ; beside, it instructed him in the school of adversity ; an academy, though not mentioned in the catalogue of education, which affords more practical knowledge than the united efforts of the most polished seminaries."

After some considerable time spent in wandering about the country, King came to London, and was fortunate enough to procure an engagement to play small parts at Drury Lane. The first part in which he appeared was that of the Younger Brother in Comus, in which he had no opportunity to show his abilities. This was followed by several other equally uninteresting and unimportant parts, and King, feeling that he was not going to have anything of a chance at Drury Lane, gave up his engagement, and crossed the sea to Ireland, where he joined Sheridan's company in Dublin.

Here he had his chance. He was cast for leading comedy parts, in which he made an instantaneous and great success.

After some years of great popularity in Dublin, he returned to London, as a result of the theatrical war which divided the Irish theatre. In London he enlisted under Garrick's banner. He was fortunate in that the esteem in which he had been held by his Dublin audiences was known to his new management, and he was in consequence able to secure a good salary, as well as parts in which he could excel.

Garrick was good enough personally to announce the play in which King was to make his first appearance, that of " The Conscious Lovers," making particular mention of the fact that " the part of Tom would be played by Mr. King, from Dublin."

He had been so many years in Ireland that his acting was quite fresh to London audiences, and he caused a furore.

In 1769, on the death of Powel, the manager of the Bristol theatre, King purchased his share of the Bristol patent, and between his share of the proceeds from this theatre, his salary at Drury Lane, and his benefit performances, his income became very considerable.

King reached the climax of his reputation in 1777, when he created the part of Sir Peter Teazle in " The School for Scandal." His style of acting was much less manieré than was usual at the time ; he was at ease and familiar in his acting, and was one of the first actors to give naturalistic and life-like performances rather than the highly stylized representations with which the audiences of the day had hitherto been familiar, and which were the common theatrical fare until the days of Kean.

He was the author of a number of successful farces, which brought him in a certain amount of money, so that, considering his large earnings on the stage and his income from his part-ownership of the Bristol theatre, as well as shares in several other smaller theatres, he should have been a rich man, but his inordinate love of gambling brought him to poverty, and he died in very reduced circumstances in 1805.

Mr Kean as Count Bertram

Mr KEAN as Richard

MR. WROUGHTON in BARNWELL.

Mr Parsons, as Col: Oldboy.

WILLIAM PARSONS

BUT LITTLE IS KNOWN of Parsons' early life, or how it was
that he came to choose the stage as a career. His first
appearance in public was at Edinburgh in the year 1758,
where he made an immediate success in a type of acting
which but few young actors choose as a suitable vehicle
for their talents, that of old men's parts. Having made
this success, Parsons was sensible enough to continue
playing such parts, which he did for several years, until
David Garrick, wanting to find an actor to play the
part of Filch in his production of the " Beggar's Opera "
in 1763, happened to have Parsons highly recommended
to him, and offered him an engagement.

Parsons accepted the offer, and managed in some way
to arrange for his wife to be engaged at the same time,
and together they made their first London appearance,

E

he as Filch and she as Mrs. Peachum. He made a great success in the part, owing to the peculiar " knowing vulgarity " of which he was master.

He continued to play old men of a low comedy type, on Garrick's advice, as he proved excellent in that type of part. A description of his acting in the part of Old Foresight in " Love for Love " explains his style of acting. " It happens with most actors who perform in disguised characters, such as buffoons, old men, etc., that, if they imitate the outlines of such a part, they are at liberty to fill it as they please ; this license often gives rise to affectation and unnatural acting ; but Parsons, by a happy attention to all the minutiae of his cast, shews a finished picture of dotage, avarice, or whatever infirmity or passions he would represent ; the tottering knee, the sudden stare, the plodding look, nay, the taking out the handkerchief, all proclaim him a finished actor in this walk." Our illustration, showing him in the part of Colonel Oldboy, gives a good idea of what is meant.

FRANCES ABINGTON

ONE OF THE GREATEST comic actresses of all time, Frances
Barton, was born in the seventeen-thirties, (the exact
date is unknown), her father having been a private soldier
in the Guards who afterwards made a living as a cobbler
in Windmill Street, near what is now Piccadilly Circus.

In after years, when she became famous, she desired to
have a rather better pedigree, and it was claimed on her
behalf that she was the great-granddaughter of Charles
Barton, of Norton in Derbyshire, and was of gentle birth.
It is impossible either to prove or disprove this statement,
so one may as well give her the benefit of the doubt.
She certainly was a woman of the greatest industry and
perseverance, and rose from very humble beginnings to
a position where she had the respect and affection of the
most distinguished men and women of her time.

After a couple of years of more or less disreputable life, (for which charity can claim that her economic circumstances and not her desires were responsible), she procured an engagement with Theophilus Cibber at the Haymarket in 1755, and appeared in various parts with much success, notably as Sylvia in " The Recruiting Officer." After some short engagements in the provinces, she was engaged by Lacy for the Drury Lane company at a salary of thirty shillings a week.

Here she found that Mrs. Pritchard and Kitty Clive had a claim to all the best parts, and in consequence she had not many opportunities for showing what she could do. Anxious to prepare herself for any chances that might come her way, however, she engaged a Mr. Abington who played in the theatre orchestra, to give her lessons in music. Despite the fact that her " cher ami," a young Creole, had spent a large sum upon her, and had promised that on his return to England, which he was just leaving for a short time, he would marry her, she only waited until his departure, (and incidentally accepted a leaving present of five hundred pounds from him as an earnest of favours to come), before marrying her music master.

This was in 1759, and almost immediately, seeing very little chance of being cast at Drury Lane for the parts she wished to play, she prevailed on her husband to resign from the orchestra, and they both went over to Ireland, where she had been offered whatever parts she liked at the Smock Alley Theatre in Dublin.

For three years she went from success to success, playing whatever leading comedy parts she preferred. Her domestic life, however, was not so successful. She formed a connection with a Mr. Needham, M.P. for Newry, which naturally enough was the cause of great jealousy on the part of her husband, although it was freely stated, (and possibly with truth), that it was a liaison of the mind alone. As a contemporary writer put it, " This connexion, brought to bear through an approving choice of the minds of both sides, rather than the gratification of any other wish, the pleasure arising from this intercourse became gradually so intense that he delighted in no company so much as her's. He enjoyed a singular satisfaction in reading, explaining, and communicating every kind of cultivation to a mind he found so happily disposed to receive and profit by his instruction."

As a result of this attachment, she and her husband agreed to part. They entered into a legal agreement whereby she covenanted to pay him a certain sum per year as long as he did not come near her. He lived some years in receipt of this pension, and then disappeared altogether from history.

In 1762 Needham was called to England to attend to business affairs, and Mrs. Abington resigned from the Dublin company, and accompanied him to Bath. There his health, which had not been good for some time, rapidly deteriorated, and he shortly died, leaving her a considerable sum of money.

Left with neither husband nor lover, she went back to her profession, and was offered an engagement by Garrick at Drury Lane, where she remained for fifteen years, mounting from one pinnacle of success to another, though not without continual squabbles with Garrick, in which truth compels one to admit the blame was invariably hers.

In 1779 Mrs. Abington created the part of Lady Teazle in Sheridan's famous play, which afterwards became one of her greatest successes. Three years later she left Drury Lane in consequence of the management's inability (or possibly merely unwillingness) to pay her the increase of salary she demanded. She was already in receipt of a thousand pounds a season, which was an enormous sum for a leading woman in those days.

She negotiated for some time with Covent Garden and at length a bargain was struck. She made her first appearance there in November, 1782, in "The Discovery," speaking an address to the audience after the first act, probably of her own composition.

> Oft have I come, ambassadress in state,
> For some poor author, trembling for his fate;
> Oft has a generous public heard my prayer,
> And shook with vast applause the troubled air.
> Then why should I, a creature of your own,
> Born of your smiles, and murdered by your frown,
> On this occasion fear your hearts can harden,

Though a noviciate now at Covent Garden ?
In short, good folks, though I have changed my school ,
Alike you'll find me here to play the fool.

At Covent Garden she remained for nearly eight years,
and retired from the stage in 1790 without the formal
leave-taking which was then customary.

Boaden wrote of her :

" She, I think, took more entire possession of the stage
than any actress I have seen ; there was, however, no
assumption in her dignity ; she was a lawful and graceful
sovereign, who exerted her full power and enjoyed her
established prerogatives. The ladies of her day wore
the hoop and its concomitant train. The spectator's
excercise of the fan was really no play of fancy. Shall
I say that I have never seen it in a hand so dexterous as
that of Mrs. Abington ? She was a woman of great
application ; to speak as she did required more thought
than usually attends female study. Far the greater
part of the sex rely upon an intuition which seldom
misleads them ; such discernment as it gives becomes
habitual, and is commonly sufficient, or sufficient for
common purposes. But commonplace was not the station
of Abington. She was always beyond the surface ;
untwisted all the chains which bind ideas together, and
seized upon the exact cadence and emphasis by which
the point of the dialogue is enforced. Her voice was of
a high pitch, and not very powerful. Her management

of it alone made it an organ ; yet this was so perfect that we sometimes converted the mere effect into a cause, and supposed it was the sharpness of the tone that had conveyed the sting. Yet, her figure considered, her voice rather sounded inadequate ; its articulation, however, gave both strength and smartness to it, though it could not give sweetness. You heard her well and without difficulty ; and it is the first duty of a public speaker to be intelligible. Her deportment is not so easily described ; more womanly than Farren—fuller, yet not heavy, like Yonge, and far beyond even the conception of modern fine ladies."

J. W. DODD

AUDIENCES OF THE nineteen twenties will remember the magazine programme, in which different actors and actresses were invited to give details of their lives, their favourite parts, their tastes and dislikes, and so on, so that the readers might not only have something to occupy their attention during the intervals, but also that the popularity of the artist about whom they were reading, might be increased by the feeling that in some sort he and they were acquainted.

This is no new thing. In 1772 three small booklets were issued, giving similar details (though, as would be expected at such a time) in rather fuller form, of the leading members of the companies at the three Theatres Royal.

The details of Dodd's career are written in so amusing a style that I make no apology for quoting from it at length, in the hope that it may prove interesting to my readers to see how a theatrical press-agent of those days, whatever he may have been called, tried to increase the popularity of his clients.

" There is scarcely a walk on the stage that the audience are more pleased with, nor one less generally understood, than that of a coxcomb. A pert vivacity, a quaintness of style, and impudent familiarity, so constitute this character, that to the gross of an audience who are not able to separate breeding from affectation, it passes for a fine gentleman. To mark this strongly, so (as in the language of painters) to make the correction obvious, must belong to an actor at the top of his profession.

Whether Mr. Dodd is indebted most to application or art, for reaching this point, we cannot determine. If we would hazard a critique founded upon general observation, we would say both ; as excellence in any profession is readiest attained by the former assisting the latter. For however we would disclaim art as the mistress, as the handmaid she is essentially necessary to be consulted.

The little hero of these memoirs was early drawn to the stage by that dazzle which the tinsel of the profession generally gives to young minds. Born in London under the immediate protection of the Muses, he became their devotee whilst at a grammar-school in Holborn ; but what confirmed him in an opinion which inclination had begun, were the compliments he received on his playing the part of Davus in the ' Andria ' of Terence, a little before he left school. These were irresistible, and soon decided him to strike at the stage, as the grand object from whence he was to derive his future happiness and emolument.

At the age then of sixteen (a period when the generality of boys are getting through the classics) we find Mr. Dodd ' facing the naked eye of an audience.' The first part he played in public was Roderigo, in an itinerant company at Sheffield ; a part which he went through with such success, as flattered his warmest inclinations ; and as the general run of country companies are not very strong in numbers, Mr. Dodd was so encouraged by this first onset, that he occasionally undertook the principal characters in tragedy : here likewise he met with equal success ; but how deservedly may very well be imagined by those who know the almost unattainable summit of universality ; an height only reached by one, who has been no less elegantly than justly styled, ' though little, yet the map of men.'

As soon as his summer's expedition was over at Sheffield, he proceeded to Norwich, where he settled for some time. Here he extended his parts in comedy, and at the same time extended his reputation ; however, he did not seem to lose sight of the buskin, as he occasionally took it up with a degree of satisfaction almost inseparable from young performers ; and meeting no discouragement from his audience to rebate a passion for a walk to which he was never called by nature, he divided his attachments between the comic and tragic muse.

Mr. Dodd continued thus no inconsiderable servant of all work, till his engagement with Mr. Arthur, master of the Bath company. The superior applause he met with in comedy from this audience (which vies with London for criticism and politeness) led him to debate this question, ' which was most to his advantage, to be considered a middling general player, or an excellent comedian ? ' Prudence, and the love of fame, fixed him to declare for the latter ; and from this time forward he cultivated his comic talents with such assiduity, as not only gained him the general approbation of the Bath audience, but encouraged Messrs. Garrick and Lacy to engage him at a genteel salary, at Drury Lane.

In the winter of 1765 he made his first appearance there in the character of Faddle, in Mr. Moore's ' Foundling ; ' nor could any performer be happier in the choice of a part, as every line of it seems written to express that particular style of acting Mr. Dodd is in the possession of. Under so excellent a judge as Mr. Garrick, there was little to be apprehended (from the specimen he gave of his abilities) that he would be improperly cast ; that great manager, as well as actor, saw the line of his merit, and gave it every judicious latitude it would bear ; till by degrees, he has produced a performer who gives no inconsiderable consequence to his company.

As an actor, Mr. Dodd, in the airy, genteel coxcomb, certainly claims originality. There are many other parts in low comedy, and as a singer, in which he is very useful, but in this we think he stands alone ; his voice, manner, and above all, his figure, is happily suited to express that light dégagée vivacity, so necessary to finish this character. We are sensible, however, that there are some critics who laugh at propriety of figure, particularly Churchill, who says :

> Before such merit all distinctions fly,
> Pritchard's genteel, and Garrick's six feet high.

But notwithstanding such authorities, we will rest it on the judgment of any impartial spectator, whether the extreme bulk and unwieldy figure of Mrs. Clive in the part of Phillis in the ' Conscious Lovers,' did not belie the idea he had conceived of Steele's Chambermaid."

What would an actor of today give for such a write-up in a programme ? or better still, in a Sunday newspaper ? Especially when it was in the general view of those best qualified to judge, a true report ? Let me quote Lamb's view of Dodd's abilities, written long after.

" Few now remember Dodd. What an Aguecheek the stage lost in him ! Dodd was *it*, as it came out of nature's hands. It might be said to remain *in puris naturalibus*. In expressing slowness of apprehension, this actor surpassed all others. You could see the first dawn of an idea stealing slowly over his countenance, climbing up by little and little, with a painful process, till it cleared up at last to the fulness of a twilight conception—its highest meridian. He seemed to keep back his intellect, as some have had the power to retard their pulsation. The balloon takes

75

less time in filling than it took to cover the expansion of his broad moony face over all its quarters with expression. A glimmer of understanding would appear in a corner of his eye, and for lack of fuel go out again. A part of his forehead would catch a little intelligence, and be a long time in communicating it to the remainder."

Dodd was not only a comic actor, but a man of merry wit off-stage. Elsewhere Lamb says of him, " Dodd was a man of reading, and left at his death a choice collection of old English literature. I should judge him to have been a man of wit. I know one instance of an impromptu which no length of study could have bettered. My merry friend, Jem White, had seen him one evening in Aguecheek, and recognising Dodd the next day in Fleet Street, was irresistibly impelled to take off his hat and salute him as the identical Knight of the preceding evening with a ' Save you, Sir Andrew.' Dodd, not at all disconcerted at this unusual address from a stranger, with a courteous half-rebuking wave of the hand, put him off with an ' Away, Fool '."

THE BADDELEYS

AMONG THE MINOR functionaries attached to the Court of King George II was a Sergeant-Trumpeter. The holder of this important sounding post was a certain Mr. Snow, concerning whom but little is known save that he was the father of a very famous woman, one of the finest actresses, and openly profligate women who graced – and disgraced – the stage in England in the latter half of the eighteenth century.

This daughter, Sophia, was remarkable for her beauty, as well as for her unusually fine voice ; two facts which tended to make her interested in the stage while still a child. The theatrical profession appealed to her as being the one which held out the greatest prospects of utilising her two gifts to some real financial benefit, and she haunted the theatres and made the acquaintance of as many of the players as she could. During this time she met the man she was afterwards to marry.

This man, Baddeley, had originally been a cook, but being dissatisfied with his prospects, engaged himself as a valet to a gentleman who was about to make the Grand Tour. While in France he picked up a smattering of the language, together with a certain knowledge of continental habits and manners, which afterwards was to stand him in good stead. On his return from the Continent he managed to procure an engagement at Drury Lane, then under the management of Garrick, where he made an instantaneous success.

As the result of a casual meeting with Sophia Snow, he fell passionately in love with her, and she with him, which made it easy for him to suggest to her that they should elope. She was only too ready, and they ran away and were married. Baddeley's salary, however, was not sufficient for the two of them to live in the style to which by this time he had accustomed himself, and he looked round to see how he could increase his income without too much trouble.

Sophia's beauty of face and form, added to her lovely voice, gave him the brilliant idea of putting them to a more profitable use than merely to pleasure him, and he arranged for her to adopt his own profession. Though entirely without training in the art of acting, she made an appearance in 1764 in the part of Cordelia in " King Lear." This appearance was quite fortuitous ; the actress who was to

TAMERLANE.

Borralet ad viv del.   Walker sculp.

Mr PALMER as BAJAZET and
M.^{ifs} HOPKINS as SELIMA.

Baj. *Now, now thou Traitrefs.* Act 5.

Published Decr 21. 1776. by T. Lowndes & Partners.

VENICE PRESERVED.

Edwards ad viv del.   Published 14 Dec.r 1776, by T.Lowndes&Partners.   Collyer sculp.

Mr BENSLEY in the Character of PIERRE

Who's he disputes the Judgment of the Senate?
Presumptuous Rebel.———   Act 4 Sc.2.

Mrs Abington in the Character of Lady Harriet.

Dodd del.   Taylor sc.

I can as ingenuously as I should then, acknowledge
that I have been in an Error.   Act.II.Sc:2.ᵈ

Published by Harrison & Cᵒ. 1ˢᵗ June 1780.

Mr King in the Character of Marplot.

Thieves! Thieves! Murder!!

Act IV.

Publish'd by I. Wenman Jany 1.st 1777.

have played the part was suddenly taken ill, and no sub-stitute for her was available in the theatre but the untried Sophia. She was pressed into service to read the part, and an unexpected incident was the cause of her great success. This was the entrance of Edgar as Mad Tom ; Sophia had never seen the play rehearsed, and the figure and manner of Tom when she looked up and saw him reeling towards her, gave her such a shock that she screamed in fright and fainted. The unrehearsed effect was so fine that it was received with loud applause.

Her acting powers, however, were not yet ripe, whereas her voice was already in its full beauty. She was in con-sequence engaged as a singer at Vauxhall Gardens, and afterwards at Ranelagh, at the excellent salary of twelve guineas a week, but she soon returned to her real love, the stage.

For three years she and her husband lived together amicably enough, working together at Drury Lane, where her charm and ability in playing comedy parts soon made her an established favourite. It was not in Sophia's character, however, long to be satisfied with so monotonous a possession as a husband, and her " affaires " with all and sundry who presented themselves soon became so flagrant that even her fellow-artists were concerned. As an anonymous author put it, writing in 1772, " The public indulgence Mrs. Baddeley gave to her gallantries, and the husband's glaring concessions, and sometimes assistance to them, roused even the delicacy of the Green Room ; and a

F

remonstrance of their being so very heedless of appearances, began to be loudly talked of by the whole company ; Mr. George Garrick entered into their resentments ; and happening to express himself, one morning, rather too warmly on this subject to Mr. Baddeley, the affronted husband sent him a challenge, which very fortunately was decided next day at Hyde Park as bloodless as those fought behind the scenes of old Drury."

There is an entertaining account of this duel in the " Town and Country Magazine," from which I quote :

" The world have been so ill natured as to suggest that Mrs. B – y had formed a connection with the late Mr. H – d : and that Mr. M – z has since been his happy successor. These reports, whether true or false, occasioned some altercation between Mr. B – y and his wife ; and, through resentment, he received her salary, without accounting to her for it.

Mr. G – e G – k remonstrated with Mr. B – y upon his conduct, which so much displeased him, that he wrote a letter of complaint upon the occasion to Mr. D – d G – k. This epistle being shown to Mr. G – e G – k, he strongly resented it the next time he saw Mr. B – y, who, thereupon, challenged him. In consequence whereof (after Mr. D – d G – k had ineffectually endeavoured, for nearly three hours, to dissuade his brother from this hostile design), Mr. G – e G – k engaged Mr. S – s, the attorney, for his second ; and Mr. B – y had sufficient influence over his supposed rival, Mr. M – z, to induce that gentleman to become his second.

These preliminaries being adjusted, they repaired to Hyde Park, and the seconds having marked out the ground, Mr. B – y had already fired at his antagonist, when his wife, who had received intimation of the affair, flew upon the wings of love (that is, in a hackney coach), to the field of battle ; and, arriving at this critical time, threw herself upon her knees ; and, whilst she looked very languishing (but whether at her lover or at her husband is not certain) cried out ' Oh ! spare him ! spare him ! ' which entreaty, it is imagined, induced Mr. G – k to fire his pistol in the air, and a reconciliation took place."

After three years of somewhat disturbed matrimonial life, Sophia and her husband separated by mutual consent. They continued to play together at the same theatre, but spoke to each other not more than their parts required. About the time of the separation Baddeley claimed his wife's salary, a claim which, though legally justified, she quite naturally resented.   This claim caused such a turmoil in the theatre that they were both dismissed from the company, and it was rumoured that on account of their notorious immoralities they would never be taken back ; but either on account of their professional abilities, or because Baddeley ceased to press his claim, they were both re-engaged the following season.

The fact that the two spouses were not on speaking terms was not long unknown to the public, and one famous day, when King George III and Queen Charlotte were present at a performance of " The Clandestine Marriage " in which Mrs. Baddeley played Fanny, and Baddeley, Canton, the situation caused a loud laugh, in which the King and Queen joined. The next day Sophia received a command from Farmer George to go to Zoffany and have her portrait painted in the character of Fanny. This royal patronage naturally increased her popularity, and her favours were desired by a still a greater number of the " rakes " who hunted for prey in theatrical circles.

Among her many suitors was a certain young nobleman who had only seen her on the stage, and had not yet made her acquaintance. He wrote an impasioned letter, begging for an interview ; she was agreeable, and made an appointment to meet him in – of all places in the world – King Henry VII's Chapel in Westminster Abbey ! The interview accordingly took place, but the lovely Sophia rejected his suit. This, however, did not prevent him making her a little present of three hundred pounds ; whether this was intended as an advance on future favours, we do not know. The meeting ended in their going round the Abbey together on a sight-seeing tour, spending a considerable time in looking at the wax-works, with which, as Sophia afterwards said in recounting the incident, they were vastly pleased.

Perhaps her most noteworthy characteristic, apart from her complete lack of moral sense where the relation of the sexes was concerned, was her insane prodigality. Although

at times she made an enormous income, she spent every
penny she could lay hands on, and never at any time stood
more than a few pounds ahead of utter destitution. Not
that she spent everything upon herself ; such was by no
means the case ; all she had was at the service of her
friends, and even of her slightest acquaintances, who, as one
may imagine, were not slow to take the fullest advangage of
her generosity.

Her character, however, showed other good points
beside her generosity ; she was passionately fond of animals
and in particular of cats. Is there something in theatrical
life which causes a love for these creatures ? It will be
remembered that Rich, the celebrated Manager of Covent
Garden, always kept several dozen cats which accompanied
him wherever he went.

Mrs. Baddeley's favourite went by the name of Cuddle,
and he always travelled with his mistress on her journeys,
sitting on her lap in her coach. On one occasion when
travelling to Portsmouth, the coach overturned, and was
dragged some considerable distance on its side before the
postboys were able to cut the traces. In the midst of all
the confusion and shouting, Mrs. Baddeley's sole concern
was for Cuddle's safety, calling out that if he was injured
she would go mad. Such affection was rewarded by the
fact that neither Cuddle nor any of the other occupants of
the coach, were even grazed on the accident.

Baddeley is chiefly remembered by his will, in which he
left the reversion of his house at Molesey to found an asylum

for decayed actors, adding the provision that when the value of the property reached £550 per annum, pensions were to be granted to the inmates.

He also bequeathed the interest on £100 to provide the company at Drury Lane with wine and cake in the green room on Twelfth Night. The custom is still observed.

JOHN PALMER

IN JOHN PALMER we see an excellent example of a man who triumphed over all difficulties and discouragements, and at long last succeeded in his chosen profession. He was born about the year 1742, in or near Old Street, in the City, the son of a private soldier.

His father had served under Lord Granby, who recommended him for the position of doorkeeper at Drury Lane. The boy became stage-struck, and asked David Garrick to give him a hearing, which Garrick good-naturedly did. Jack recited to him the parts of George Barnwell and Mercutio, but the actor saw no ability in him, and urged him to follow his father's profession, and enlist.

The boy, feeling that thus he would be carried further away from his chosen path, refused to take Garrick's advice, and obtained instead a job in a print-seller's shop on Ludgate Hill.

At a benefit performance for the theatre staff, in which his father was included, he was given the part of Buck in " The Englishman in Paris." As a result of this, he was engaged by Foote for the Haymarket, where in 1762 he created the part of Harry Scamper in Foote's " Oracle." He then joined a provincial company for a short while, and returned to London, where he appeared as George Barnwell in " The London Merchant," (the part which he had originally read to Garrick), at another benefit performance for his father. He was re-engaged by Foote, but soon dismissed. David Garrick, apparently feeling pertinacity should be rewarded, engaged him for Drury Lane at a salary of a pound a week, to play small parts.

In 1764 he created the part of Sir Roger Dowlas in Foote's " Patron," after which he again went into the provinces, joining Hurst's company at Colchester. In Norwich he married a Miss Berroughs, who had been greatly attracted by him, and had taken a box at his benefit performance.

A year later he was engaged again by Garrick for Drury Lane, at a five shilling increase on his former salary, which, on Palmer's remonstrance that he was now a married man, as well as a more experienced actor, he raised to thirty shillings a week. At the Lane he was billed as " J. Palmer " to distinguish him from another member of the company, the elder John Palmer, known as " Gentleman " Palmer.

Here Palmer was disabled for some considerable time by an accident on the stage. When playing Dionysius in the " Grecian Daughter " to Mrs. Barry's Euphrasia, the spring in her dagger failed to work, and she wounded him severely.

After a further engagement at the Haymarket, Palmer went in 1772 to Liverpool, to succeed Thomas King. There he became a great favourite, but later lost a great deal of his popularity when rumours began to circulate that he grossly ill-treated his wife. It seems probable that there was a good deal of truth in them. He sent for his wife, who, it is said, hid the bruises that he had inflicted on her, and was seen walking in the streets of Liverpool with him in amicable converse in order to re-establish him with the public.

He returned to London in 1776, and appeared again at the Haymarket, where he created the part which was to become his greatest success, that of Joseph Surface, in " The School for Scandal." In this part he was universally admitted to be without an equal.

His remarkable ability in parts of this kind is more easily understood when it is known that his nickname was " Plausible Jack." A story is told that after a disagreement with Sheridan, the author of " The School for Scandal," Palmer in his best " Joseph Surface " manner, said " If you could see my heart, Mr. Sheridan." Sheridan replied " Why, Jack you forget I wrote it ! "

Charles Lamb wrote of him, " In sock and buskin there

was an air of swaggering gentility about Jack Palmer. He was a *gentleman* with a slight infusion of *the footman* . . . When you saw Jack figuring in Captain Absolute, you thought you could trace his promotion to some lady of quality who fancied the handsome fellow in his topknot, and had bought him a commission." (One would fancy that Lamb had some knowledge of the circumstances of his marriage !) " Jack had two voices, both plausible, hypocritical, and insinuating ; but his secondary or supplemental voice still more decisively histrionic than his common one. It was reserved for the spectator, and the *dramatis personae* were supposed to know nothing at all about it. The *lies* of Young Wilding, and the *sentiments* in Joseph Surface, were thus marked out in a sort of italics to the audience. This secret correspondence with the company before the curtain (which is the bane and death of tragedy) has an extremely happy effect in some kinds of comedy."

In 1785 Palmer built the Royalty Theatre in Wellclose Square, against the advice of all his friends, because he had only received licenses from the Governor of the Tower, and the local magistrates. Consequently it could only be used for the performance of pantomimes and similar pieces, and he became involved in perpetual strife with the managers of the patent theatres. He fell head over heels into debt, and was imprisoned for a time within the Rules of the King's Bench.

His death was tragic. He was announced to play in Liverpool in " The Stranger." Very depressed through the loss of his wife, to whom he had become reconciled, as well as that of the favourite child of all his large family, he did not feel up to appearing, but nevertheless did so. He played the first two acts with all his accustomed ability, but faltered in the third. In the fourth act, when he had to reply to a question in the play relative to his children, his emotion overcame him, and he fell back, dead. The audience supposed he was playing his part, and it was not until they saw his body removed that they knew the tragedy that had been enacted before their eyes, and that the English stage had lost one of the most versatile actors who had ever graced it.

It may be of interest to know that Palmer's ghost is supposed to have appeared after his death.

PRISCILLA HOPKINS

PRISCILLA HOPKINS, whose portrait is here seen with Palmer, playing the part of Selima to his Bajazet in " Tamerlane," was born in the year 1756, the daughter of the prompter at Drury Lane Theatre. Her mother was an actress in Garrick's company, and at the age of nineteen Priscilla appeared with her as Mildred in " Old City Manners," an adaption of " Eastward Ho ! "

She next played the part of Fanny in " The Clandestine Marriage," and created the part of Maria in " The School for Scandal," in which she made a decided hit.

While playing at Drury Lane, she fell in love with another member of the company, William Brereton, a man fifteen years older than herself, who was not of very stable intellect. Brereton went to Dublin in 1785, where he attempted suicide, as a result, it was believed, of a hopeless passion for Mrs. Siddons. He recovered, but for the rest of his life, which mercifully only lasted another two years, he was kept in close confinement at Hoxton.

A few months after Brereton's death, Priscilla married the famous John Philip Kemble, with whom she appeared in a number of plays. In 1796, however, at the early age of forty, she took her final farewell of the stage, preferring a life of quiet domesticity, which lasted for a further half century. She had no children, and on her death just before her ninetieth birthday, her property was divided among the Kemble and Siddons families.

She was extremely pretty, gay and piquante in her acting, but she had no great histrionic ability. Genest says of her that she was " seen to most advantage in parts like Maria in the " School for Scandal."

ELIZABETH YOUNGE

" DESCENDED FROM A GOOD FAMILY, who left her little beside her education, the heroine of this page had her situation in life to make at a period when most girls are occupied by no other ideas but their pleasure. Before she had time to determine on any thing, a dignified professor of the long robe paid his *devoirs* to her. This gentleman, being early bred an apothecary, and afterwards pursuing the law, (with whose quibbles he soon became very conversant) it is not to be expected he should be a connoisseur in the mysteries of Cupid. Plutus, however, was his friend, who prevailed so feelingly with the young lady, that, on certain conditions, she condescended to bless his arms. For some time, from the force of gratitude on her side, and novelty on his, this amour was supported with a tolerable grace ; but short is the date of that connexion where the hearts do not unite ! The natural moroseness of his temper breaking out, removed the artificial affection she was induced to shew him ; and despising a settlement so imcompatible with happiness, she readily dissolved a connexion, to which her hand, not her heart, consented."

Such was the florid way in which a contemporary stage writer explained the disastrous marriage of Miss Younge. To enable her to earn a living in the way she preferred, she procured an introduction to Garrick, who was much taken with her appearance and abilities, and trained her for the stage.

In the winter of 1768 she made her first appearance as Imogen in " Cymbeline," in which she showed great promise. She had played a number of important parts under Garrick's management, when she received an excellent offer from the Smock Alley Theatre in Dublin. Garrick permitted her to accept it, and in 1771 she went to Ireland, where she made an enormous success. This success resulted in Garrick's becoming aware of his having let a swan escape from his pond, and he asked her to return to Drury Lane, which she did, there equalling the success she had enjoyed in Dublin.

She married Alexander Pope, an Irish actor and painter, nineteen years younger than herself, who was a leading member, first of the Covent Garden, and then of the Haymarket companies, for many years.

She was an actress of unusual versatility, the part in

Mrs. Abington in the Character of Corinna.

O Lord, a letter! is there ever a token in it?

Act 2.d Scene 1.st

Terry Sculp.

Publish'd by J. Harrison & Co. 1 Nov.r 1778.

Miss Younge in the Character of Merope.

And I will kneel a wretch and thank your justice.

Act IV. Scene 1.

Publish'd by I.Wenman March 1ˢᵗ 1777.

Roberts del   Publish'd as the Act directs Decr 29th1777.   Thornthwaite Sc.

Mr *GARRICK in the Character of* **ABEL DRUGGER**.

Engraved by W.P. Sherlock.

Mrs Garrick

From the Original Picture by Cath. Reid,
in the possession of S. Edwards Esqr.

ELIZABETH YOUNGE

which she was best known being that of Merope, in which
she is shown in our illustration. I quote from the only
contemporary notice of her which I have been able to
see, which gives a clear account of how she appeared
to her audience.

" Her person is happily suited to the dignity of tragedy,
being perfectly well made ; and though not an absolute
beauty, her face and address are both agreeable. Though
her voice is not exactly tuneable, it is far from being
discordant, particularly in tragedy, where her conduct
of it takes off all its harshness. This lady is likewise much
indebted to nature for a pliancy of features, that mark the
passions she would present with great expression. She
should guard, however, against the excess of this requisite,
as by too frequent a repetition it loses its force, and consequently its utility."

G

JAMES AICKIN

" THOUGH THIS GENTLEMAN happens to have nothing very particular in his history, his merit as an actor, and his rank on the stage, oblige us to open a niche for him in the temple of theatrical biography." With these words an anonymous contemporary opens an account of Aickin's career.

He was the only son of a wealthy weaver in Dublin, who designed him as his successor in the business, but the boy's predilection for a theatrical life was so marked, that after serving a short apprenticeship to his father, he abandoned all claim to a business life, and went on tour with a travelling company in his native land.

He made his first appearance in the part of George Barnwell, in which he made a certain success, but although the country audiences were highly appreciative of his talents, he found the life of an itinerant player not at all to his

97

taste, and applied for, and gained, an engagement at the Smock Alley Theatre in the capital.

The Smock Alley house at this time, in common with most of the Dublin theatres, was not in very good financial circumstances, and the management found it advantageous to assign the principal roles to those of the company who could afford to play " on credit," rather than to those who demanded their money with promptness and regularity. The latter were penalised by being cast for parts which their dignity and professional standing would not allow them to accept, with the hoped-for result that they resigned their engagements.

This was the case with Aickin, and he would no doubt in any case have gone to seek pastures new, had it not become essential for him to do so for quite other reasons. In the year 1764 he fell in love with a lady of considerable fortune, but of a different religion. This being, in Ireland – then as now – an almost insuperable bar to matrimony, he arranged to the public celebration of matrimony, he arranged to carry her off, with her willing consent. For this purpose a night was chosen, and Aickin with a few close friends was supping at a tavern in the neighbourhood of his lady-love's abode, preparatory to the elopement. They invited an Englishman, a stranger to them all, who was supping there, to sit at their table and join them in their meal.

As the arranged hour drew near, Aickin, who had been keeping his courage up by frequent draughts of claret, developed a passionate attachment to the stranger, whom he had never seen until an hour or two before. Being unable to bear the pain of parting from this new-found friend, he said he would give him an immediate proof of his deep feeling for him. Pulling out a case of pistols from his pocket, he said, " Know, my dear boy, I'm engaged to run away with a lady this night, supported by these gentlemen ; you shall be of my party, -- here " (pointing to the pistols) " are the poppers ; come away, we have not a minute to spare."

The stranger, who, fortunately for himself, was sober, being alarmed at the suggested exploit, did not at first know how to excuse himself, until suddenly an idea occurred to him. He told Aickin he was vastly obliged to him for so great a proof of his friendship, and that he would value nothing more than the opportunity of attending him on his interesting excursion, but that he had injured his leg a few days before, and would be unable to run, which might be the means of discovering the party.

This excuse was accepted by Aickin, who then hurried off with his friends, reached his loved one's house, and satis-factorily concluded the elopement. He and his wife, however, had the good sense not to remain in Ireland, and crossed over at once to London, where he secured an engage-ment at Drury Lane, and rapidly made a name for himself on the London stage.

Aickin's forte lay in the more impassioned and declama-tory parts of tragedy, from which circumstance he was nicknamed " Tyrant " Aickin. Though his vein was essentially that beloved of Bully Bottom, whose " chief humour was for a tyrant : he could play Ercles rarely, or a part to tear a cat in, to make all split," yet in private life his character was quite the reverse ; he was gentle and kindly, and a most generous friend to those who needed his help.

ROBERT BENSLEY

ROBERT BENSLEY WAS BORN about the year 1738, and is believed to have started life as a Lieutenant of Marines, and to have seen active service in America. According to his own statement, which, however, must be received with a certain caution, Garrick saw him playing in an amateur performance, and at once gave him an engagement.

However it was that he procured an engagement, he certainly did make his first professional appearance on the London stage at Drury Lane, where in October, 1765, he played the part of Pierre in " Venice Preserved." He remained under Garrick's management for two years, appearing in such Shakespearean characters as Edmund in " King Lear " and Buckingham in " Richard III." He then transferred to Covent Garden, where he appeared off and on for eight years, and in 1775 he returned to Drury

Lane, where he played during the winters, appearing at the Haymarket during the summer seasons.

In 1796, the death of a relative, Sir William Bensley, placed him in the position of a gentleman of independent means, and he left the stage after his benefit performance of " The Grecian Daughter," in which he played Evander to the Euphrasia of Mrs. Siddons.

But little is known of his private life. He is said to have married a lady with whom he fell in love as the result of his accidentally being the means of her being thrown from her horse.

Regarding his professional ability, his contemporaries do not seem to be in complete agreement. O'Keefe says of him that he was " an exceedingly well-informed, sensible man . . .as an actor he was most correct to the words and understood his author," an excellent example of damning with faint praise !

Lamb, however, had the greatest admiration for his talents. The fact that he has universally been considered the greatest of all Malvolios, none too easy a part to play without turning him into a figure of fun, makes it seem probable that his abilities were of no mean order.

I quote Lamb's description :

" Of all the actors who flourished in my time . . . Bensley had most of the swell of soul, was greatest in the delivery of heroic conceptions, the emotions consequent upon the presentment of a great idea to the fancy. He had the true poetical enthusiasm—the rarest faculty among players. None that I remember possessed even a portion of that fine madness which he threw out in Hotspur's famous rant about glory, or the transports of the Venetian incendiary at the vision of the fired city. His voice had the dissonance, and at times the inspiriting effect, of the trumpet. His gait was uncouth and stiff, but no way embarrassed by affectation ; and the thorough-bred gentleman was uppermost in every movement. He seized the moment of passion with greatest truth ; like a faithful clock, never striking before the time ; never anticipating or leading you to anticipate. He was totally destitute of trick and artifice. He seemed come upon the stage to do the poet's message simply, and he did it with as genuine fidelity as the nuncios in Homer deliver the errands of the gods. He let the passion or the sentiment do its own work without prop or bolstering. He would have scorned to mountebank it ; and betrayed none of that *cleverness* which is the bane of serious acting. For this reason, his Iago was the only endurable one which I remember to have seen. No spectator, from his action, could divine more of his artifice than Othello was supposed to do. His confessions in soliloquy alone put you in possession of the mystery. There were no by-imitations to make the audience fancy their own discernment so much greater than that of the Moor—who commonly stands like a great helpless mark, set up for mine Ancient, and a quantity of barren spectators, to shoot their bolts at. The Iago of Bensley did not go to work so grossly. There was a triumphant tone about the character, natural to a general consciousness of power ; but none of that petty vanity which chuckles and cannot contain itself upon any little successful stroke of its knavery—as is common with your small villains, and green probationers in mischief... The part of Malvolio, in the " Twelfth Night," was performed by Bensley with a richness and a dignity, of which (to judge from some recent castings of that character) the very tradition must be worn out from the stage. No manager in those days would have dreamed of giving it to Mr. Baddeley, or Mr. Parsons ; when Bensley was occasionally absent from the theatre, John Kemble thought it no derogation to succeed to the part."

RICHARD WROUGHTON

RICHARD WROUGHTON WAS BORN IN 1748 in the city of Bath, and while training for the profession of a surgeon, made several appearances on the stage in his native city. This bred in him such a desire for stage fame, that he gave up all idea of medicine, and went to London, followed by a young milliner who had fallen in love with him, and had nursed him through a serious illness. They were married in London, and he was fortunate enough to be engaged by the management of Covent Garden, where he made his first appearance as Zaphna in " Mahomet."

He apparently showed little ability during his first season, but by sheer hard work developed into a competent actor, and was re-engaged for a second season, during which he improved so much in his craft that he received a long contract, and in fact remained at Covent Garden for seventeen years.

About the year 1777 he became part proprietor with Arnold of Sadler's Wells, but sold his share in 1790.

In 1787 he joined the Drury Lane company, where he made his first appearance as Douglas in " Percy," afterwards playing Hamlet, Antonio in " The Merchant of Venice," Sir Peter Teazle, Henry IV and Richard III.

He retired from the stage in 1798, and went to live in his favourite Bath, but two years later, Palmer having died and Aickin being ill, the management of Drury Lane begged him to come back and help them. He did so, and continued with them, on and off, for a further fifteen years. His last performance was in his old part of Withers in Kenney's " World."

Seven years later he died in London, and lies buried in St. George's, Bloomsbury.

Kelley in his " Reminiscences " refers to him as being " A sterling, sound, and sensible performer." He seems rarely to have reached any great heights in his acting, but his common-sense and ability saved him from being dull. Despite the natural disadvantages under which he laboured, being knock-kneed, with an inexpressive face and an uninteresting voice, he was able in a great measure to overcome his defects, and gained a large measure of appreciation from public and managements alike.

SARAH SIDDONS

" BORN IN THE PROFESSION " is a phrase frequently heard of an actor. Remarkable indeed it is, how much more often the son or daughter of theatrical parents adopts those parents' profession as his own, than is the case with the children of those of other professions.   Of all the girls born to the profession of the stage, Mrs. Siddons undoubtedly takes first place.   She was the daughter of Roger Kemble, manager of a theatrical company, and his wife, Sarah Ward, and made her first appearance before the public at so early an age that she was but just able to speak.

An interesting tale is told of her first appearance.   Her father and mother, who were at the time in serious financial difficulties – by no means a rare event in their lives – were to have a benefit performance, and the little Sarah was led onto the stage by them, in order to make an additional appeal by her childish charm. The child's presence, however, had quite a different effect from that fondly anticipated by her parents ; the taste of the audience was offended at the sight of so tiny a mite appearing on the stage, and an uproar ensued. The little one, being frightened, ran towards the wings, when her mother caught her and brought her forward to the footlights, whispering to her not to be afraid, and telling her to repeat to the people a story she had learnt by heart, the fable of the Boys and the Frogs. The appositeness of the story was greeted by the audience with loud cheers, and the situation was saved.

By the time the child was twelve years old, she had already sung in a number of operas, and had made a considerable name. In her fifteenth year the precocious girl fell violently in love, her choice falling upon an actor in her father's company. Her parents, somewhat naturally, did not smile upon the suit, not fancying a penniless and none too successful actor in the role of son-in-law, and incontinently removed Sarah from the stage, placing her as lady's maid with a Mrs. Greathead, who lived in Warwickshire, at a sufficiently great distance from her disconsolate and abandoned swain.

At the age of seventeen she fell in love again, this time in earnest, with a Mr. Siddons, who was acceptable to her parents, and marriage shortly ensued. Very soon after the wedding she reopened her theatrical career by appearing at a theatre in Cheltenham, where she was fortunate enough to gain the admiration of the Earl of Aylesbury, a connoisseur in matters theatrical, and a man of considerable taste. He recommended her to Garrick's notice, who, being unable at the moment himself to visit Cheltenham, deputed a friend, the Rev. Henry Bate (afterwards better known as Sir Henry Bate Dudley), to see here in various characters, and report to him as to her abilities.

Mr. Bate saw Sarah play a number of parts, and was greatly taken with her, particularly in the part of Rosalind, in which she excelled. So highly did he esteem her as an actress that he wrote to Garrick, urging him to engage her. She made her first appearance under Garrick's management when she was twenty years old, playing the part of Portia in " The Merchant of Venice."

Her debut, however, was a complete failure, for which her youth and inexperience, her stupid choice of parts, and the jealousy of the already established actresses in the company, were responsible. She was refused a re-engagement, and, depressed and miserable, had to return to the scenes of her provincial successes. For her children's sake, however, she did not long mourn her vanished opportunity, and in order to earn money was compelled to begin once again the drudgery of the life of a country actress, playing for the most part in Bath.

At long last, more than six years after her inglorious defeat on the London stage, she again had a chance of achieving metropolitan laurels. She received an offer from Drury Lane, which she accepted. On beginning rehearsals, however, she was attacked by such nervousness that she was hardly able to speak. When the great night came, a vast audience had gathered to see her. The play was " The Fatal Marriage," in which she appeared as Isabella. She was supported by a number of well-known artists, among whom were the well-established favourites, Farren and Palmer ; her old father, Roger Kemble, was also hovering about to give moral support to his beloved daughter. Her husband, it is reported, could not face the strain of the evening's performance, but walked the streets until the play was finished.

The evening was a tumultous success, and her fame as a great tragedienne was assured. She herself wrote of it : " I reached my own quiet fireside on retiring from the scene of reiterated shouts and plaudits. I was half dead, and my joy and thankfulness were of too solemn and overpowering a nature to admit of words or even tears. My father, my husband, and myself sat down to a frugal meat supper in a silence, uninterrupted except by exclamations of gladness from Mr. Siddons. My father enjoyed his refreshments, but occasionally stopped short, and laying down his knife and fork, lifting up his venerable face, and throwing back his silver hair, gave way to tears of happiness. We soon parted for the night, and I, worn out with continually broken rest and laborious exertion, after an hour's retrospection (who can conceive the intenseness of that reverie ?), fell into a sweet and profound sleep, which lasted to the middle of next day. I arose alert in mind and body."

Now for a secret, worth twenty pieces.

Act 3.^d Scene 2.^d

Tory, Sculp.

Publish'd by J.Harrison & Co Pr March 1780.

De Wilde pinxt.   Leney sculp.

Mrs SIDDONS as ISABELLA.

This ring was the first present of my love
To Biron my first husband.

London, Printed for J. Bell, British Library, Strand, May 26, 1792.

JOHN BULL AT A COMEDY.

Published 8th March 1796 by LAURIE & WHITTLE, 53 Fleet Street, London.

169

EFFECTS OF TRAGEDY.

Published as New Guide by LAURIE & WHITTLE, FLEET STREET, LONDON.

From that moment Mrs. Siddons never looked back. She followed her success as Isabella with the part of Euphrasia in " The Grecian Daughter," and then played, in rapid succession, Jane Shore in the drama of that name, Calista in " The Fair Penitent," and Zara in Congreve's " Mourning Bride." At the end of the season she crossed to Dublin, where she appeared with her brother, John Kemble, and made an enormous success.

On her return to London, she paid a visit to Dr. Johnson. As might be imagined from what we know of her character, she greatly pleased the crusty old man, who wrote in a letter to Mrs. Thrale, " Mrs. Siddons, in her visit to me, behaved with great modesty and propriety, and left nothing behind her to be censured or despised. Neither praise nor money, the two powerful corrupters of mankind, seem to have depraved her. I shall be glad to see her again. Mrs. Siddons and I talked of plays, and she told me her intention of exhibiting this winter the characters of Constance, Katherine, and Isabella, in Shakespeare." Of this visit a pretty little story is told. When she came into the room, there happened to be no unoccupied chair. " Madam," said Johnson, " you who so often occasion a want of seats to other people, will the more easily excuse the want of one yourself."

Of all the parts played by Mrs. Siddons, there is no doubt that it was in that of Lady Macbeth that she excelled. In his " Lives of the Players," John Galt gives an excellent description of her performance in this role. " She entered,"

H

he writes, " according to the tragedy, reading the letter. It was evident by her manner that Lady Macbeth had previously seen something in the letter which had so affected her, that she had instinctively come forward two or three paces from the spot where she had first opened it. But when she came to ' they made themselves air,' she paused for an instant, as if doubtful of the term employed, and then uttered the word ' air ' in a tone of wonder. From that moment her voice assumed a more earnest accent, and I would say the demon of the character took possession of her . . . The magnificence of her descent from the throne at the banquet was another example of the previously inconceivable sublimity of the genius that directed her conception of the part ; and perhaps, as such, was not inferior to her somnambulism. Whether her action in the dream scene – that brightest spark of the poet's fire – was according to the phenomenon of the disease, I would not examine ; for it was so tremendous, that, with such a character, gnawed with the Promethean agonies of crime, it ought to have been natural."

One tale concerning her is so well known that it hardly seems necessary to retell it, but it may be worth doing so for the sake of any who have not heard it. One day, at supper at a tavern, Mrs. Siddons wished to explain to the waiter that he had mistaken her order. She was so accustomed, however, to speaking in blank verse, that ordinary prose was for the moment beyond her powers, and the astonished waiter heard her roll forth in the manner of high tragedy, the immortal line :

" You brought me water, boy ; I asked for beer ! "

It was as Lady Macbeth, the part in which she made her greatest success, and in which she has never been surpassed, that she took her leave of the stage in the summer of 1812. An event occurred on this occasion which was without precedent in theatrical history. After Lady Macbeth's final exit, the play was discontinued, the audience making it clear that their purpose that evening was to see, and say farewell to, Mrs. Siddons.

She appeared only twice after her formal farewell, once at her brother's benefit performance in 1816, and again the same year by Royal Command ; with these two exceptions she remained faithful to her decision to say a final good-bye to the stage whilst still comparatively young. She died at her house in London in June, 1831.

GEORGE FREDERICK COOKE

GEORGE FREDERICK COOKE was born in the year 1756 in
barracks in Ireland, the illegitimate son of an army officer.
According to his own account, he was born in Westminster,
but there is very little doubt but that his version of the tale
is without the slightest foundation.

The boy and his mother, soon after the father's death,
which occurred when he was little more than a baby,
went to live in Berwick, and at the age of eleven young
Cooke saw his first play, " The Provoked Husband."
As soon as his sketchy education was finished, he was
apprenticed to a printer, but soon broke his indentures,
and went to sea as a cabin-boy. He soon grew weary
of the sea, and returned to Berwick, where he managed
somehow or other, to make sufficient money to stay for
a while in London.

In 1774, after he had reached the capital, he saw the great David Garrick, then on the verge of retirement, in all his principal characters, and nothing would do him but to try to emulate the master. He managed to get an engagement with a strolling company which was playing at a public house in Brentford, where he made his debut as Dumont in " Jane Shore."

From the first his genius showed itself, and it was not long before he became a great favourite with provincial audiences. What was afterwards to become the great curse of his life, however, that of violent dissipation, already began to show itself. When sober, he was a brilliant actor, but his periods of sobriety became less and less frequent. When the drink fever was on him, he would become a complete animal, haunting the lowest quarters of whatever town he happened to be in, and becoming more and more degraded week after week. This meant that often he was unable to appear in the play for which he was billed, and audiences which had paid hard-earned money to see him, were hard to pacify when they learned the reason for his absences. But his great ability always led to his forgiveness by a faithful public.

In November, 1794, Cooke appeared for the first time in Dublin, in the part of Othello. In the middle of the season he suddenly vanished, and nothing whatever was known of him until 1796, when he equally suddenly reappeared in Southampton. The reason for his disappearance was what might be imagined. A great and

glorious round of dissipation had culminated in his enlist-
ment in the army, when he was too drunk to know what he
was doing. His regiment was due to go to the West Indies,
but, fortunately for him, Cooke was kept behind owing
to an illness. The managers of the theatre at Manchester,
old friends of Cooke, purchased his discharge, and sent
him sufficient money to get to Manchester. Instead of
expending it on the journey, however, he drank it all,
and was ashamed to ask his benefactors for more. Ill as
he was, and suffering from the effects of a long bout of
drinking, he managed to get as far as Portsmouth, where
he got into communication with Maxwell, manager of
the theatre there. Maxwell advanced the money a second
time, and arranged with the managers of the Manchester
theatre that he should be put on the coach for London,
met there, and transferred to the Manchester coach.

His reappearance on the Manchester boards being
hugely advertised, a large crowd gathered in the theatre
to greet him. They were disappointed, however, for
despite all the precautions that were taken, he failed to
arrive. But he did come a few days later, and eventually
appeared as Octavian in " The Mountaineers," and the
audience forgave his outrageous treatment of them on
account of his superb acting.

Later in the year he returned to Dublin, where he played
a long season, appearing also in Cork and Limerick.
His career in Ireland was chequered with frequent bouts
of drunkenness, in one of which he challenged a man

to fight him. His opponent refused the challenge, on the grounds that it was against his principles as a poor man, to fight a rich one. Cooke promptly threw his pocket-book which contained a large sum of money in notes, on the fire, and said, " Now I don't own a farthing. Come on ! "

In 1800 Cooke reached the summit of his career, with the offer of an engagement at Covent Garden. This offer he accepted, and the following year he made his first appearance in what was to become his great part, Richard III. The season was a remarkable one for Cooke, for not only did he win the greatest possible success in the parts he played, but he also managed to keep sober throughout, a unique feat throughout the course of his life.

Such sobriety, however, was more than could be expected to last. Cooke went on a successful provincial tour in Scotland and the North, and (presumably owing to unwillingness to leave the neighbourhood of good Scottish whiskey), he remained in the North, playing at the Newcastle theatre on the very night when he was due to make his reappearance at Covent Garden.

When he did eventually reappear, he made a profound apology to the justly irritated audience, who, moved by the power of his acting, accepted his regrets. Unfortunately, heavy drinking which prevented him from appearing after he had been announced for a part, became more and more frequent. He was constantly too " indisposed " to play, and on making his apologies, his references to " his old complaint " were greeted with roars of ironical laughter.

In June, 1810, he made his last appearance in London, and shortly afterwards sailed for New York to fulfil an engagement which he had made to appear there under Thomas Cooper's management. This engagement he had made, incidentally, without any regard to the fact that he had already contracted to appear at Covent Garden for the forthcoming season, as well as to one if not two provincial managements. Cooper was accused of having enticed him away when he was drunk. As the moments when he was not drunk were very few and far between, there was probably a certain amount of truth in the accusation.

In the October he sailed on the " Columbia," and at once embarked on an orgy of drink. He mercifully suffered badly from sea-sickness, and when he was able to appear on deck again, his companions had drunk every drop of drink on board ! Consequently, when the boat arrived at New York, he was completely sober, and a few days after his arrival, still sober, he appeared in his great part of Richard III, and made a colossal success. Continual sobriety was, of course, too much to expect, and when he staggered on to the stage for the third performance, he was too drunk even to be audible.

In June, 1811, only seven months after his arrival in the United States, he was attacked by dropsy, brought on by his fearful excesses. His drink-sodden frame gave him no chance against the ravages of the disease, and he died in September of the same year, at the age of fifty-five.

Poor Cooke ! Despite his terrible weakness, the cause of his sudden death, he must have been a most likeable man. No one without immense charm could risk constant appearances when too drunk even to speak, and yet always be forgiven. But he was a genius ; and they are perhaps not to be judged as ordinary men.

JOSEPH MUNDEN

EARLY IN THE year 1758 there was born in the neighbourhood of Leather Lane, a spot no more salubrious then than now, a baby boy, destined to become one of England's greatest comedians.

Joe Munden was the son of a poulterer, and as soon as the boy was old enough he had to help out the family fortunes by working as an assistant at an apothecary's. Whatever talent he may have had as a chemist's assistant, however, paled into insignificance before a fresh gift which was evidenced in the course of his work, that of an unusually fine handwriting. The little Joe was in consequence apprenticed to a Mr. Druce, a law stationer, who had a shop in Chancery Lane.

Propinquity, as ever, was the cause of love; and the near neighbourhood of Drury Lane brought a temptation to the boy that was quite irresistible. He was a fervent admirer of the great Garrick, and used often to run away from home, and attach himself to some band of strolling actors, in the hope that he might some day join his idol in his chosen profession.

But this fancy of Joe's was not at all relished by his family, and every time he ran away, his mother used to go after him and fetch him back. One day, however, he got clean away, and went to Liverpool, where, owing to his beautiful handwriting, he got a job in the Town Clerk's office at the magnificent salary of half-a-guinea a week. This he supplemented by appearing as an extra at the theatre at eighteenpence a night.

After some time at Liverpool, he gave up his job, and made his way to Leatherhead, where he was engaged to play old men and character parts in a strolling company. The barn in which the company played was burnt down— a frequent happening, owing to the use of candles—and Munden's penmanship again came in handy in writing a petition which was sent all round the neighbourhood, and brought the management the sum of nearly thirty pounds.

The unfortunate actors and actresses did not get much benefit from it, however, for the manager paid each of them five shillings on account, and when morning came, was nowhere to be found.

This misfortune did not damp Munden's ardour, and he found engagements with other strolling companies at Wallingford, Windsor and Colnbrook, where the manager again decamped with the takings. This time poor Joe thought he had had enough, at any rate for the present, and returned home like the prodigal son.

Like the prodigal son, too, his father and mother received him with open arms, hoping that he would now be satisfied to stay, but the theatre was the breath of life to Joe, and he soon fixed an engagement at the Haymarket. There he was seen by the manager of the Canterbury theatre, who suggested that he should join his company.

His feet were now firmly on the ladder of success, and from the moment of his engagement at Canterbury, he never looked back. From Canterbury he went to Brighton, from there to Chester. One of the partners in the Chester theatre meditating retirement, a friend, out of admiration for Munden's ability, offered to lend him sufficient money to buy the partnership. Munden accepted the offer, and in a remarkably short time had done so well that he was able to repay the whole sum.

But, alas! Joe was no more proof against the shafts of love than any one else, and fell in love with a girl in the company, a certain Mary Jones. He had a liaison with her for some time, and when he became a partner in the management of the company at Chester, he introduced her everywhere as his wife.

After they had been living together for nine years, and become the parents of four daughters, she suddenly became attracted by another actor, and ran away with him, taking one of her daughters with her.

The disclosure of the liaison considerably damaged Munden's reputation at Chester, and he hastened to make people forget about it by marrying in good earnest. His bride was a Miss Frances Butler, a lady of some social position, and this match succeeded in whitewashing him to some extent in the eyes of provincial society.

In 1790 Covent Garden Theatre lost its great comedian, John Edwin, through death, and Munden was offered the vacant position. He sold his share in the Chester circuit, and joined the London company, making his first appearance there as Sir Francis Gripe in " The Busy Body," and Jemmy Jumps in " The Farmer."

He remained at Covent Garden for twenty-one years, ever-increasing in fame and popularity, until in 1811 he quarrelled with the management. It must be admitted that in this quarrel he was entirely to blame, since it arose through his claim for full salary for a long time during which he had never appeared at all on the stage, having been incapacitated through gout.

He swore he would never set foot in Covent Garden again—an oath which, except when he once appeared to play at a benefit performance, he religiously kept—and joined the company at the Haymarket. Two years later he migrated to Drury Lane, where he appeared on the memorable occasion of Kean's first performance of Sir Giles Overreach in Massinger's "A New Way to pay

Old Debts." Not only the audience, but Munden himself, in the part of Marrall, were paralysed with fear during this performance, and Munden himself had to be dragged off the stage by the arm-pits, murmuring " My God! My God! Is it possible? "

In 1824, in the part which he created, old Dozey, a half-drunken sailor, in Dibdin's " Past Ten o'clock and a Rainy Night," he took his farewell of the stage. He lived for eight further years, the " carefulness " in money matters which had always characterised him, gradually turning into absolute miserliness.

All in all, he was probably the finest comedian of his type that our stage has ever known. His acting was described by Charles Lamb in these words. " There is one face of Farley, one of Knight, one (but what a one it is!) of Liston; but Munden has none that you can properly pin down and call *his*. When you think he has exhausted his battery of looks, in unaccountable warfare with your gravity, suddenly he sprouts out an entirely new set of features, like Hydra . . . In the grand grotesque of farce, Munden stands out as single and unaccompanied as Hogarth. Hogarth, strange to tell, had no followers. The school of Munden began, and must end, with himself."

In conclusion, I quote from Charles Lamb's essay, " On the Acting of Munden " :

" Not many nights ago I had come home from seeing this extraordinary performer in " Cockletop " ; and when I retired to my pillow, his whimsical image still stuck by

me, in a manner as to threaten sleep. In vain I tried to
divest myself of it by conjuring up the most opposite asso-
ciations. I resolved to be serious. I raised up the gravest
topics of life ; private misery, public calamity. All would
not do :

> There the antic sate
> Mocking our state . . .

his queer visnomy, his bewildering costume, all the strange
things which he had raked together—his serpentine rod
swaggering about in his pocket—Cleopatra's tear, and the
rest of his relics—O'Keefe's wild farce, and *his* wilder com-
mentary—till the passion of laughter, like grief in excess,
relieved itself by its own weight, inviting the sleep which in
the first instance it had driven away.

But I was not to escape so easily. No sooner did I fall
into slumbers, than the same image, only more perplexing,
assailed me in the shape of dreams. Not one Munden, but
five hundred, were dancing before me, like the faces which,
whether you will or no, come when you have been taking
opium—all the strange combinations, which this strangest
of all strange mortals ever shot his proper countenance
into, from the day he came commissioned to dry up the
tears of the town for the loss of the now almost forgotten
Edwin. O for the power of the pencil to have fixed them
when I awoke ! A season or two since, there was exhibited
a Hogarth gallery. I do not see why there should not be a
Munden gallery. In richness and variety, the latter would
not fall far short of the former . . .

M^r. Moody as Teague.

Upon my soul I believe he's dead.

Act 4th Scene Ist.

Publish'd by Harrison & C°. April 1.1779.

Terry sculp

Mrs Barry in the Character of Sir Harry Wildair.

Here is a nest of the prettiest goldfinches
that ever chirp'd in a cage

Act II. Scene 2.

Published by I. Wenman 1 Sepr 1777.

Mr Barry in the Character of Othello.

This only is the Witchcraft I have us'd.

Act I. Scene 3.

Publish'd by I.Wenman Feb:y 1777.

Can any man *wonder*, like him ? can any man *see ghosts*, like him ? or *fight with his own shadow*—as he does in that strangely-neglected thing, the " Cobbler of Preston "— where his alternations from the Cobbler to the Magnifico, and from the Magnifico to the Cobbler, keep the brain of the spectator in as wild a ferment, as if some Arabian Night were being acted before him. Who like him can throw or ever attempted to throw, a preternatural interest over the commonest daily-life objects ? A table or a joint-stool, in his conception, rises into a dignity equivalent to Cassiopeia's chair. It is invested with constellatory importance. You could not speak of it with more deference, if it were mounted into the firmament. A beggar in the hands of Michael Angelo, says Fuseli, rose the Patriarch of Poverty. So the gusto of Munden antiquates and ennobles what it touches. His pots and his ladles are as grand and primal as the seething-pots and hooks seen in old prophetic vision. A tub of butter, contemplated by him, amounts to a Platonic idea. He understands a leg of mutton in its quiddity. He stands wondering, amid the commonplace materials of life, like primaeval man with the sun and stars about him."

EDMUND KEAN

IN THE YEAR 1787 was born a child, who was destined by
Fate to become the greatest actor known to the British
stage, Edmund Kean. He was the illegitimate son of
Aaron Kean and Nance Carey, two small-part actors,
who left him to be brought up by a member of the Drury
Lane Company, a Miss Tidswell, whom he called his
"Aunt Tid."

His mother apparently cared nothing for him, and was
only too delighted to be relieved of the care of him. From
his father he inherited nothing but his raven-black hair,
his wonderfully magnetic eyes, and the streak of madness
and dissipation which was to wreck his fortunes in later life.

He made his first appearance on the stage at the age of
three, when he appeared in a ballet at Drury Lane. Of
his childhood we know little, save that it was unhappy.

While still quite a boy he had to earn his own living, and since his foster-mother was on the stage, it was only natural that he should turn to her profession as that in which he could best make a start.

He was fortunate enough to procure an engagement in Samuel Jerrold's company, and immediately lost his heart to Mary Chambers, an Irish girl who was also a member of the same company. She reciprocated his feelings, and at the age of twenty he became her husband.

A few months after their marriage he accepted an engagement to play in Swansea, and as they were quite penniless, they started to walk there from London. Mrs. Kean was shortly to have a baby, so the journey was not an easy one for her. At length, footsore, ragged and hungry, they arrived in Swansea, where Kean, procuring an advance of a few pounds, attempted to forget his troubles in a round of drink and dissipation. This was unfortunately to be his habit to the end of his days.

At Swansea the leading man was an extremely bad actor called Smith. One of Kean's first parts was that of Polonius to Smith's Hamlet. Smith was so incredibly bad, not to say funny, in his playing of the part that Kean thought he might as well be funny too, and in the middle of one of the gravest scenes, turned a somersault. The manager naturally enough called on him to explain his conduct, and Kean, truthful as always, said that Smith was so comic that he thought Hamlet was being played as a farce, and that consequently Polonius should be comic as well! Extraordinary to relate, Kean's explanation was accepted, and more extraordinary still, on the removal of Smith, Kean was promoted to play the leads in his place.

Through the instance of a kind friend, Arnold, stage-manager of Drury Lane, came to see Kean, and offered him a three-year engagement at the Lane at a rising salary of eight, ten, and twelve guineas a week, to play leading parts, a proposal which Kean eagerly accepted. When the directors of the theatre met him, they were disappointed with his appearance, which had nothing remarkable about it except for the big, flashing, black eyes, and suggested that it might be wiser for Kean to agree to play smaller parts until he became known to the audience. But Kean was not at all agreeable to do so; for leads he had been engaged, and leads he would play.

The story of his first appearance at Old Drury as Shylock has often been told. He only had one rehearsal before playing the part, and was censured by the stage-manager during the rehearsal, who said that it would never do, since Shylock had never been played in that way before.

" Sir! " said Kean, " I may be wrong, but if so the public will set me right."

The night came, and it is reported that so little did any of the company think of him, that not a soul spoke to him except the call-boy. No one wished him luck; complete and utter failure was confidently anticipated. Not only did the supporting actors feel jealous of the newcomer, but he had gone out of his way to flout tradition, which, as always, they felt as a personal insult—he wore a *black* wig, instead of the ginger one which had been worn by generation after generation of Shylocks.

His opening words made the audience realise that a new star had arisen, and by the time of the scene with Tubal, containing the famous lines:

" I had it of Leah when I was a bachelor: I would not have lost it or a wilderness of monkeys! "

the unutterable pathos with which Kean spoke them was so electrifying that the small audience was worked into a positive frenzy of excitement. Many of them rushed out during the interval, and brought in friends with them to see an actor the like of whom they had never seen before. At the fall of the curtain Kean's triumph was complete. He dashed back to his lodgings, an attic in Cecil Street, Strand, and burst in on his wife with the words, " Mary, you shall ride in your coach, and Charley shall go to Eton."

The directors of the theatre, to their everlasting credit, tore up Kean's contract, and gave him another with an enormous increase of salary. In quick succession he played Richard III, Hamlet, Othello, Iago, and Duke in " Riches." It is reported of him that the only revenge he took for the cool reception he received from the stage-manager and company of the Lane when he first arrived, was to ask the said stage-manager, one Raymond, to share a bowl of punch. Raymond accepted with alacrity, whereupon Kean emptied the bowl over his head.

After a short season in Dublin, where he met with the greatest success, he made his reappearance at Drury Lane, again playing Richard III. This he followed by playing Macbeth, in which he was not able to repeat his former complete triumph. Like the egg, it was " good in parts." He then appeared as Romeo, a part which he himself disliked and thought unsuitable, but which he undertook at the particular request of the management. " But," he said to his wife, " I'll disappoint them in it, damned if I don't." And he did. He was totally unsuited to the part of a young lover, though in the death scene his tragic power was so great that he could not fail to succeed.

The next part he attempted was that of Richard II. This was the first time that the play had been produced since shortly after Shakespeare's death, and it had been " adapted for the stage " by Wroughton, a contemporary actor, who did not hesitate to cut it about and give dialogue assigned by the author to one character, to another. As the weak king, Kean was a failure. He was too strong and passionate in his portrayal of emotion for such a character. But there must have been something in his performance that redeemed it, for he drew vast audiences to see him play the part.

After a further period of provincial appearances, came the most astonishing tour-de-force of his career. Early in 1816 Kean persuaded the management of the Lane to put on Massinger's famous old play, "A New Way to Pay Old Debts," which he wished to use as a vehicle for showing his power of frightening an audience by his portrayal of a villain.

The performance when it came off was noteworthy. Kean's acting as Sir Giles Overreach reached heights of terror never before scaled upon the stage. A number of the audience had to be removed in hysterics; Lord Byron, who was present, had a convulsive fit; many of his fellow-actors collapsed from fear, and were unable to complete the performance; while Joe Munden, who was playing Marrall, had to be dragged off the stage by his arm-pits, murmuring " My God! My God! Is it possible? "

To the member of a present-day audience it might well seem impossible that one man's acting could have had such an effect; but there is too great a weight of evidence as to what happened, for us to disbelieve it.

The management and the company were so struck by the incredible power of Kean's performance as Overreach, that they subscribed to present him with a silver cup, which was formally handed to him by Robert Palmer, the oldest member of the company. Kean made a delightful speech in reply, in which he expressed his great appreciation of the fact that the presentation was made at the hands of one who had played with Garrick and the giants of the theatre, and yet did not disdain the talent, such as it might be, of the present generation.

The years went by, Kean having success after success, together with one great failure, when he appeared as

Mr. Garrick in the Character of Bayes.

There's a bold flight for you non!

Act. IV. Sc. 2.

Publish'd by I. Wenman April 1 1777.

MR KEAN AS LEONATUS POSTHUMUS,
in
Cymbeline.

Orestes, in which he attempted to rival the great Talma, whom he had seen play the part in Paris.

In 1818 the management of the Lane had what Kean called the " audacity and effrontery " to offer him the part of Joseph Surface in " The School for Scandal." He returned the part at once in a most high-handed fashion, saying that he " never had, never did, and never would " play seconds. Incidentally it is interesting to notice that never, not even in his barn-storming days, did he play anything but leads.

The unpleasantness which this incident led to was quickly cleared up, and shortly afterwards Kean, in the role of Lear, made what was to be the last great success of his amazing career. With the one exception of Hazlitt, who had disagreed with Kean about the version of the play to be used, all the critics agreed that never before had such a performance been seen.

At the end of the season, which he concluded by appearing in his famous part of Richard III, Kean sailed for America, and made his first appearance in New York on November 29, 1820, again as Crookback. The theatre was besieged by crowds for days, and the takings were higher than had ever before been known.

While in New York, Kean saw his way to combining a kindly action with a good piece of publicity. George Frederick Cooke, it will be remembered, had died in New York, and had been buried in the strangers' burial ground of St. Paul's Church. Kean had Cooke's remains removed to a more prominent part of the grave-yard, and erected over them a column bearing an inscription stating that it was erected to the memory of Cooke by Edmund Kean " of Drury Lane," ending with a horrid little piece of doggerel, composed by himself, and of which he was vastly proud,

> " Three kingdoms claim his birth,
> Both hemispheres pronounce his worth."

When Kean arrived back in London, he was annoyed to find that he was announced to appear the same evening as Richard III. But finding out that it was caused by misunderstanding a letter in which he had given the date of his return, he consented to play, and his success was as great as ever. Later in the season he appeared as Othello, and made his last appearance on October 30, at a performance commanded by the unhappy Queen Caroline. It was at this performance that the Queen was seized with her last illness, of which she died a week later.

During a further visit to America it became sadly evident that Kean was drinking far more than was good for him, and the peculiarities to which this led were now beginning to be increased by occasional attacks of insanity. Insanity and genius, alas! are seldom far removed from each other. He began to be homesick for England, and late in 1826 he sailed from New York for the last time. Early the following January, Kean appeared again at Drury Lane in the part of Shylock, before an enormous audience. He gave a magnificent performance, but at the end of it was seen to be completely worn out.

He again played Othello and Richard III, and – though it was apparent that his memory was failing him – it was thought that he might manage to attempt a new part. He was therefore announced to appear in Grattan's " Ben Nazir." A huge audience gathered to see him in a new role, but when the evening came Kean was unable to remember two consecutive lines of his part, and the curtain fell in silence.

His remaining years were tragic. A quarrel with his son Charles, whom he attempted to prevent following in his own footsteps as an actor, was succeeded by a quarrel with the management of Drury Lane, which resulted in his leaving the company, and joining that at Covent Garden, where he appeared under the management of John Kemble. There he remained for the rest of the season, playing all his greatest successes, but not attempting any new parts. While on holiday in Scotland, he became reconciled with his son, who was playing in Glasgow. Kean agreed to play at Charles' benefit, the father in the part of Brutus and the son in that of Titus, in " The Fall of Tarquin." Both played magnificently, the applause was enormous, and Kean whispered to his son, " We are doing the trick, Charles! "

In the autumn Kean returned to London, beginning the season as usual with Richard III. He was so much better that he attempted a new part, that of Virginius in

Sheridan Knowles' version of that play, in which, surprisingly enough considering the state of his memory, he scored a considerable success. He then went for a short tour in Ireland, supported by his son, and played in Dublin, Belfast, and Cork.

His farewell appearance was made at Covent Garden on March 25, 1833, when he played Othello to his son's Iago. He was dreadfully weak, and had to be supported to the wings. He was not in any condition to be acting at all, but bravely struggled on, as far as the great speech of farewell, which he spoke with such a depth of feeling that the audience burst into wild applause of minutes' duration.

His last words on the stage were prophetic. " Farewell! Othello's occupation's gone! " Kean collapsed in the arms of his son, who carried him from the stage. He rallied sufficiently to be taken down to his home at Richmond, where on May 13 he died. He was buried at Richmond, in a grave close to that of Burbage, the original creator of so many roles afterwards played by Kean.

There he lies – the great Edmund Kean – all in all, the greatest actor that ever trod the English stage.

" We shall not look upon his like again."